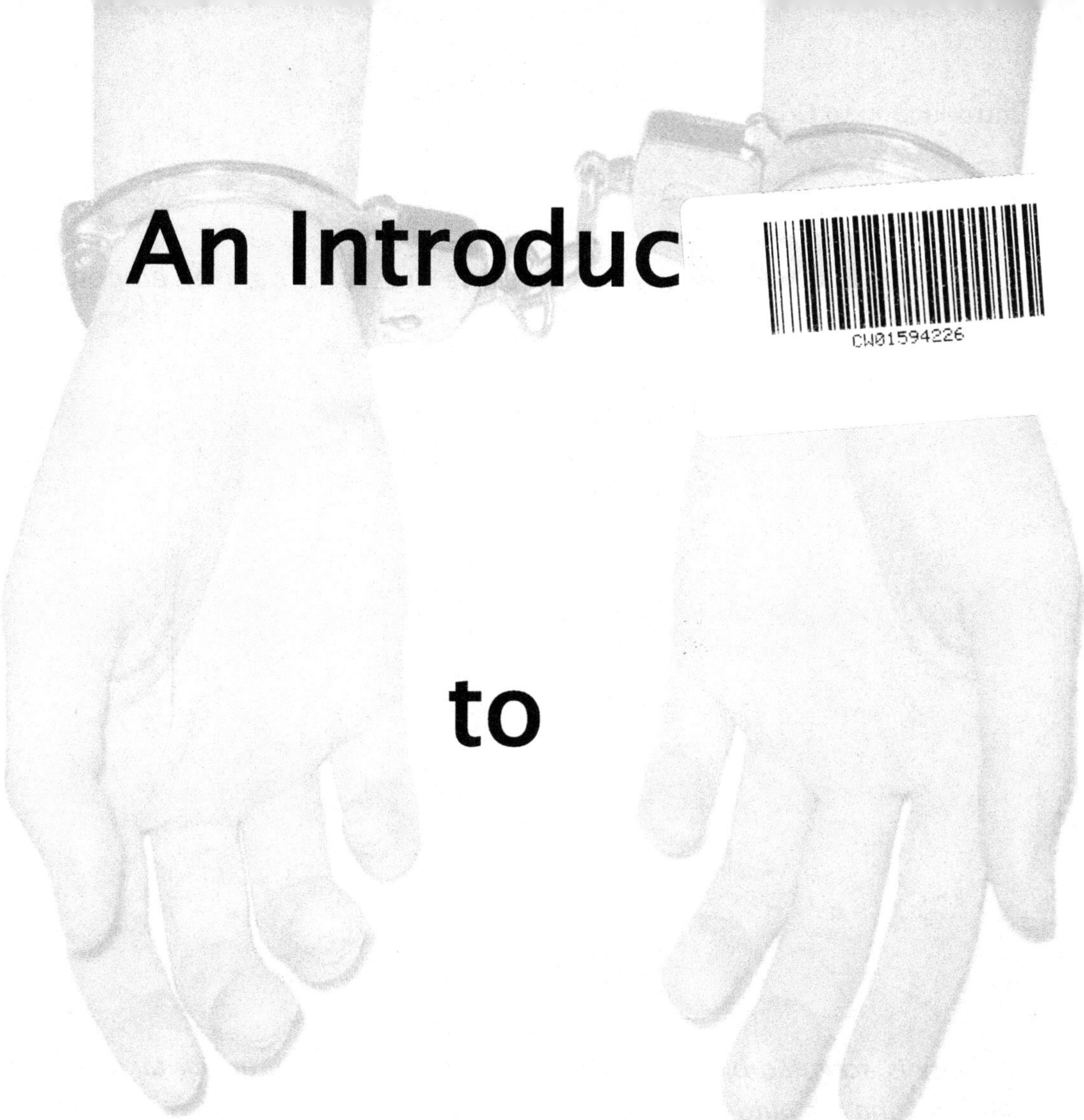

An Introduc

to

Criminology

A plain English guide to Criminology

By Teresa Clyne BA, MSc

"Dedicated to all of those who change the lives of others by empowering them for greatness." Teresa Clyne

Disclaimer:

Contents

Introduction

A beginner's guide to Criminology

This introductory guide focuses on the vital core of criminological theories— theory, method, and criminal behaviour detailed in a clear concise manner which is has at its core plain English for ease of reading and comprehension, therefore ensuring that it is straightforward and will enable readers to more fully comprehend this complex subject, it covers current topics along with historical principles and theories, these are explored to give the reader the basis to understand not only the core of criminology but to form an unbiased subjective opinion on where criminology has come from and where it is going. No one viewpoint in dominant in Criminology. A large number of theories are used when attempting to define crime, with stark differences between the "mainstream" theories and "critical" theories. Criminology is the study of crime, a "crime" is the commission of an act or omissions which is illegal. The state will punish the wrongdoers. It asks why do certain people commit crimes, what is the reason for it, why does race, gender or age have an impact on criminal behaviour? It also asks what impact crime has on society and the reactions of society to them.

Some of the questions criminologists ask and answers sought in criminology research include;

- Why do crime rates vary from time to time and from culture to culture?
- Why are some people more prone to committing crime than others?
- Why do crime rates vary across different ages, genders, and racial/ethnic groups?
- Why are some detrimental acts criminalised and not others?
- What can society do to prevent crime?

The two main theories of criminology;

Biological Theories

- Criminal are "born"

Sociological Theories

- Criminals are "made"

Conventional theories focus on predefined and set crimes, these theorist explain crimes principally in terms of individual traits and features of the immediate social environment, particularly the family, school, peer, work, and neighbourhood environments. Critical theories on the other hand use broader definitions of crime, they predominately focus on corporate and state crimes, and they explain such crimes in terms of the general social environment, particularly conflict between the rich and poor and social divides within society.

Criminologists believed there were several policies for controlling crime, including deterrence (sanctions or fines severe enough to deter offending), incapacitation (removing offenders from society so they cannot commit crimes), "imprisonment", and rehabilitation and prevention (educating and establishing ways to reduce crimes from happening in the first place).

This guide also looks at the effects crime has on society and policy decisions, and the connection between theory and criminal behaviour.

Chapter One

Crime

The most often-quoted definition of crime is that of Merriam-Webster as

> *"an act or the commission of an act that is forbidden or the omission of a duty that is commanded by a public law and that makes the offender liable to punishment by that law; especially : a gross violation of law."*[1]

Criminology

Before we explain what criminology is, we will first define what criminology is NOT. It is not the criminal justice system, how the laws are made, how the police and gardai work, it is not about prisoners and it is not about morals. Criminology is not about how the world should be, criminology is about the study of crime, what causes crime, why do individuals commit crimes, why do individuals commit crimes at certain times, this guide will also look at the social reaction to crime, and how this affects individuals who commit crimes.

Criminology is a branch of Sociology, criminology and sociology are sciences. "Scientia" is a Latin word for knowledge, criminology is in the "ology" field, ology is the study of something, therefore "crime" "ology" is the study of crime. This guide encourages you to look at the evidence, question everything you read, even what I have written, question the systems and acts, such as Mala Se and Mala Probibita crimes. "

A criminologist will attempt to examine and explain criminal behaviours; they ask such questions as, why some people commit crime and others don't?

---

[1] http://www.merriam-webster.com/dictionary/crime

A criminologist will examine such things as;

- the types of crimes committed in that society or location
- the rates of crime of crime within that society or location
- what are the different crime rates in different countries, and
- how has crime evolved over time

Criminology is a social science (*unlike physics or chemistry or physics which are natural sciences*), it is concerned with making the law, breaking the law and the consequences of breaking the law, i.e punishment.

Crimes can be categorised into two distinct fields,

"Mala in Se", these are crimes which violate societies rules, these are universal, they are obviously wrong, they are wrong or evil acts which are recognised as bad, children are thought at an early age not to steal, assault or murder etc, where they live is not important, these are moral as well as legal wrongs and therefore Mala in Se.

"Mala Prohibita" is a legal wrong, it can be more difficult to recognise, such as rules from one country to another, for instance, traffic rules may not be the same in one country as it is in another and therefore easier to breach. These can be such things as drunk and disorderly and not having a TV licence or not paying water rates, society may not see them as crimes but nonetheless they are.

Which of the following 10 acts do you consider mala in se crimes, mala prohibita crimes, or not a crime at all? Explain each one.

- possession
- vandalism
- drink driving
- sale of alcohol to minors
- fraud

- spouse abuse
- adult male having consensual sex with underaged person
- prostitution
- speeding

Criminology is the study of crime, however there is also a discipline called penology, which is the study of punishment, there is chapter later in the guide dealing with penology, and this is concerned with motivation for punishment, i.e.

- Retribution (*punishment for punishment's sake, people feel safer when an offender is punished*)
- Rehabilitation (*assisting criminals to change their ways, modern criminology and penology is looking towards rehabilitation rather than retribution in order to reduce prison numbers*)
- Deterrence (*put them off offending again, can you name a type of deterrence?*)

Criminology is a multi-disciplinary (it deals with so many different areas and topics), it has elements of psychology, sociology, medicine, law, geography and architecture. One question I ask you before we define crime further is to ask you, have you ever committed a crime? Have you partaken in any of the following?

- On your mobile phone while driving;
- Speeding;
- Parking without paying fees;
- Not putting tax on your car by the required date;
- Not buying your TV licence;
- Not paying your property tax

The list can go on, but there are few amongst us that can truly say they have never broken the law, I can however put your mind at rest, let me explain, the crimes above are what I call "*socially acceptable crimes, or socially acceptable criminal behaviour*" How often are you aghast that your friend got a speeding ticket or parking ticket?. Unlikely you would be, however, should they come into your home and tell you they have hit someone and knocked them down and didn't bother to stop, your acceptability of their criminal behaviour would stop here, wouldn't it? Can you identify when criminal behaviour stops being socially acceptable?

It could be said that "*if there is no law then there is no crime*"! Can you break down or explain what is mean by this sentence?

Antisocial, deviant and immoral conduct

Anti-social Behaviour

Section 1 of the *Housing (Miscellaneous Provisions) Act, 1997* defines "*anti-social behaviour*" as;

> *b) any behaviour which causes or is likely to cause any significant or persistent danger, injury, damage, alarm, loss or fear to any person living, working or otherwise lawfully in or in the vicinity of a house provided by a housing authority under the Housing Acts 1966 to 2002 or Part V of the Planning and Development Act 2000, or a housing estate in which the house is situate or a site and, without prejudice to the foregoing.*[2]

Deviance

Deviant behaviour is literally any conduct that differs from the prevailing norms of a specified group within society. (*acting and behaving outside what society believes is right*) A deviant will go outside societies norms, for instance, if there is a walk on the left rule in school and they walk on the right just because they do not like rules, this can be classed as deviant, or facial tattoos or purple and pink spiked hair, these are all examples of deviant behaviour. (*however, this is relative, i.e. it may be deviant in on society and not another*).

---

[2] Anti-Social Behaviour - Symptoms, Solutions, Strategies. Dr. Padraic Kenna, School of Law, National University of Ireland Galway.

Immoral and Illegal behaviour

Morals = rules of right conduct inside society, breach of these can result in social sanctions, shunning etc.

Laws = Rules which are enforced within society, breaches of these can result in criminal sanctions, fines or loss of liberty.

Let us define what is meant by illegal and immoral behaviour. For example, Murder and Rape are **immoral** and **illegal**, (*example: to take a life is immoral, but it is also illegal as it carries a criminal sanction.*)

Not all immoral acts are illegal.

- Lying
- Cheating

Not all illegal acts are immoral.

- Drink driving
- Cheating on taxes
- Smoking marijuana

We can also say that some behaviour is immoral but not illegal.

For instance in Ireland and the UK it is not a legal requirement to save the life of a stranger. If a person was walking on the beach and a swimmer go into difficulty there is no obligation on them to even attempt to save their life, they can drown and the passer-by has not breached any law, however, society and morals would dictate that those actions were immoral and wrong. Sigmund Freud believed that all humans have criminal tendencies criminals are made. It is through socialization that these tendencies are controlled during childhood.

In a nutshell, criminology examines the nature, magnitude and causes of crime.

The History of Criminology

Pre-Enlightenment Europe

Law in this time was violent and terrifying for those who sought to rely on it, when often time the victims were punished from making a complaint and even the smallest complaint could find a person thrown in prison awaiting trial. A trail which could take years or in fact never happen at all, you could be found guilty and sentenced to death with little or no proof of guilt.

Judges were given unfettered powers and offenders were often sentenced for crimes which were never in fact defined as crimes, there was no legal or formal processes or procedures in court and no legal representations were allowed to the persons accused who were normally tortured in order to obtain confessions and admit guilt,

Once the offender was found guilty the punishments were severe and swift, usually much more severe for the poor than sentences or punishments for the rich who could easily buy themselves out of trouble and even be exempt from any kind of punishments. Crime in the Middle Ages was associated with religion and demonic manipulation. In short, the best way to explain crime was the influence the devil had on society or an individual. Besides crime, natural disasters were the work of demons.

The bubonic plague (*Black Death*) which swept through Ireland in the 1300's leaving countless dead bodies in its wake was an example of demonic influences at work. During this era, deviant acts were considered to be a sin requiring harsh punishment or death. One popular form of punishment was trial by ordeal.

Medieval Trials

Trial by Ordeal

Judicium Dei (Judgement of God) or God will help the innocent.

Trial by Ordeal was used in Europe until 1220. Replaced by trial by jury.

It was used to determine the guilt or innocence of an accused person. The innocent person completed the task uninjured or their wounds would heal properly. The guilty would suffer injury or their wounds would fester.

Trial by Fire.

The defendant (accused) must walk across hot coals to retrieve an object, if they successfully get to the other side unscathed then they are innocent.

(even if they got burnt, their wound should heal quickly, within days), if it festered then they are guilty and could be sentenced to be hung, drawn or quartered.

Trial by Water.

The defendant was bound in the foetal position and thrown into water. The priest was the judge and there was the pomp and ceremony involved.

As in the public executions of the 16th Century, those that sank weren't drowned but were hauled out of the water; if he or she floated, they were guilty, and if they sank, they were presumed innocent.

Trial by Water (varying countries)

Casting the accused into water with a millstone around his/her neck – the innocent would not sink, (the weight of the crime did not press upon the innocent). Therefore the innocent were released, they guilty were removed just before they were tortured and killed.

Hung, drawn and quartered

The process began with the prisoner being placed on a wooden frame and dragged through the streets to the place of execution. On arrival they would be placed on the gallows and hung until close to death.

Now comes the not so nice part. Whilst still alive they would be cut open and disembowelled, and to add insult to injury, they would often have their private parts cut off and then be beheaded.

Trial by Hot Water

The accused would have to put their arm elbow-deep into hot water, to grasp a ring, stone, or holy object at the bottom of a pot. After several days, if no blistering or peeling was present, the defendant was presumed innocent.

Example of other Ordeals (from around the world)

Internationally there are such trails as, trial of "*Old Calabar*" (Ordeal bean) a poisonous bean, if ingested by the innocent they would survive, if guilt they would die. This was the favourite ordeal when person was accused of witchcraft.

Cangue

In china there was varying ordeals but the one that survived until modern times, the defendant was shut into a cangue, the crimes they were accused of were put on a scroll on the end, they could not eat or drink themselves, if the people around them believed they were guilty then they were not fed or given water, (*therefore guilty and would die*) this is thought to be the first form of trial by jury.

In 1220, trial by ordeal was abolished and trail by Panel was introduced. This created a new system called trial by panel. Under this principle, a group of prominent men would listen to the testimony and look at the evidence and then pronounce guilt or innocence. From this system of trial by panel we got our own system of trial by jury.

This was brought into being to give effect to natural justice, (fair, just and right). It is the ancient ancestor of our modern common law system. A jury of twelve free men were assigned to arbitrate in these disputes. Unlike the modern jury, these men were charged with uncovering the facts of the case on their own rather than listening to arguments in court.

In the 1600 compurgation was introduced (12 men who investigated the case was replaced with the pre modern 12 peers (*also removed, now 12 persons*).

In the 1700s the idea of prisons was made popular by religious orders, religious orders believed that if a person was put into a small confined room with a bible for a specific length of time they would be reborn and no longer commit crimes.

From the mid-1800s the modern criminal justice systems uses Judge and Jury. The prosecution (the *State*) would present their case and the defence (*person accused)* would present theirs. The jury would then look at the facts and decide the guilt or innocence of the defendant.

The Enlightenment age

This period marked a departure from the old religious explanation of the world and a more scientific explanation was development. Theorists opposed cruel punishments by introducing reason and science into society using. They challenged ideas which were grounded in religion and superstition. This time saw the introduction of the social contract was formed; this contract was based on the right to govern by consent of the people rather than divine consent of royalty.

The social contract basically states that citizens will be required to give up some of their freedoms to do as they please in return for a structured Police force and laws that protect everyone, the needs and rights of the many outweigh the needs of the few. The introduction of the rule of law was to follow.

It was at this time that the Rule of Law, rather than by theology was introduced. It was in this age that some astute judges began to remove some crimes from the throws of the guillotine or noose, for such crimes as petty theft or affray (*public disorder*), one particular case in 1770 whereby a mother was sentenced to death for theft, Mary Jones was hanged as a direct consequence of the law in the UK at that time that stated the government could press gang any person into service on the ships, Mary's husband was removed from the home leaving Mary without income to support her children, she was made homeless and ended up on the streets with her children, she stole some material from a clothes shop and was caught, she was sentenced to death. Her death created such uproar that more and more judges became aware of the need to differentiate crimes and seek alternative sentences.

It was at this time in the mid-1700s that some people working in State positions and power began to question the mode and methods of crime was dealt with, the slow introduction of police dealing with and preventing crime rather than the swift execution of law breakers was welcomed and the pubic hangings which many viewed as a weekly outing were condemned by Peace keeper (*Justice of the Peace*) Henry Fielding. Watchmen were set up; these watchmen were the precursor to the Police force, the first Police in the UK was made up of the Henry Fielding's Bow Street Runners and in Ireland by John de Blaquire (*Watchmen*) with the formation of both Police forces after this time by virtue of ***Wellesley's Dublin Metropolitan Police Act (1808).***

Sir Robert Peel was the home secretary who introduced in a series of Acts a central Police force; this took some time to establish but the ***Metropolitan Police Act in 1829*** established Britain's (*and Ireland's **Irish Constabulary Act (1836)***) first professional police force under the control of two police commissioners who were responsible directly to Robert Peel. The force was initially established at 3,000 men, many recruited from existing Bow Street Runners and also from ex members of the army. Peel was an advocate for change and repealed the death penalty for larceny in shops (*Mary Jones*) and on board ships; in fact he gave the judges powers to refuse the death penalty for all crimes except murder, therefore reducing the amount of executions immediately.

After Robert Peel became Prime Minister in 1835 the use of Gibbetting (*or hanging dead bodies or body parts for public display*) and Pillory (*stocks*) was abolished. Peel believed that there would be no reform in the criminal law until the Police were reformed and that crime rates would reduce when the Police lead by example not execution, the reform of the Police finally started when all counties in the Country were required to conform to a set of specific rules laid out in the ***County and Borough Police Act of 1856***.

This led to the modern judicial system, criminology, a branch of sociology (why people do what they do) which has its modern roots in classicism and positivism, which began in the late 1800's. It took some 40 years for the death penalty to be removed by all judges and some continued to order the death penalty for menial crimes and the last recorded child to fall victim to the gallows was a nine year old boy from Essex who was found guilty of arson.

According to classical criminology, humans are logical and behave in accordance with free will and rational choice. The motivation for deviant behaviour is the pursuit of pleasure (Hedonistic) while avoiding pain.

This led to the belief that in order to deter crime, the pain of punishment must outweigh any pleasure that may be gained. This principle highlighted that the criminal justice system failed to consider how personal circumstances influenced an offender's criminal behaviour.

Chapter two

The Classical School

The Classical theory was developed in response to the corrupt, arbitrary, and harsh systems of criminal justice that existed in Europe during the 1700s. These laws were often vague, with bribery of judge's commonplace and punishments for the same crime varied widely between offenders depending on tier class or ethnicity, punishments were often quite harsh, involving torture and death. This is when the Classical theory wanted to replace this system with one that was more fair and just. They claimed that people are rational and pursued their own interests, in order to maximize their pleasure and minimize their pain. People choose to engage in crime when they believed that the proceeds of the crime will bring more pleasure than pain of any punishment, therefore the classical theorists contended that the best way to control crime is to ensure that the pain of punishment outweighs the pleasure of crime, but only if the punishment was swift, severe and certain, meaning that all laws should be the same for everyone and punishment fitted the crimes.

Classic criminology began with the view that human behaviour was rational and claimed that people have the ability to choose right from wrong.

Cesare Beccarria and Jeremy Betham who were concerned about the criminal justice system and its shortcomings were the advocates in the Classical School. Classicism believed that criminality and the administration of criminal justice were based on principles of rationality, choice, responsibility, and the deterrent power of punishment. (Beccarria).

The roots of rational choice theory go all the way back to these classical theorists, the central points of their theory are:

The human being is a rational actor,

1. Rationality involves an end/means calculation,
2. People (freely) choose behaviour, both conforming and deviant, based on their rational calculations
3. The central element of calculation involves a cost benefit analysis: Pleasure versus Pain [hedonistic]
4. Choice, with all other conditions equal, will be directed towards the maximization of individual pleasure,
5. Choice can be controlled through the perception and understanding of the potential pain or punishment that will follow an act judged to be in violation of the social good, the social contract,
6. The state is responsible for maintaining order and preserving the common good through a system of laws (this system is the embodiment of the social contract),
7. The Swiftness, Severity, and Certainty of punishment are the key elements in understanding a law's ability to control human behaviour. (Keel, R. 1997)

This went against the former belief that deviant behaviour was attributed to heredity or demonic possession. Beccarria and Bentham also advocated for less cruel forms of punishment.

Rational Choice

Rational choice theory focuses on the situational aspects of criminal behaviour and stresses that a criminal rationally chooses both the crime to commit and the target of the crime.

Rational choice can be explained as an event that occurs when an offender decides to risk breaking the law after considering his or her own need for money, personal values or learning experiences and how well a target is protected, how affluent the neighbourhood is or how efficient the local police are.[3]

N.B. There are numerous perceptions of behaviour from the point of view of the criminal, I will deal with three. Perceptions of crime from a criminals point of view, criminals when questioned on their criminal behaviour tend to state some of the following as their interpretation at the time of the commission of the offence, they tended to;

- overestimate the money they receive from crime,
- they is no choice, legitimate work is not available,
- they are overly optimistic about getting away with their crimes.

(***Example:*** *This theory is also known as the situational theory; this explains that each person uses choice in deciding whether or not to commit a crime. i.e. they weigh the proceeds of the criminal act against their perceived punishment "if" they get caught.*)

Rational choice theorists are concerned with the conditions which promote crime and enhance criminality within society. It is also about reducing crime by reducing the opportunities to commit crime.

---

[3] Cornish, Derek B. and Ronald V. Clarke 1986 "Situational prevention, displacement of crime and rational choice theory." In Kevin Heal and Gloria Laycock (eds.), Situational Crime Prevention: From Theory Into Practice. London: HMSO

Cesare Beccaria (1738-94).

Cesare Beccaria focused on 18th-century law; he was an advocate of the social contract theory (these were the legal protections people had to against crime, they gave up certain freedoms in return for state protection.), he believed in guilt and punishment, this punishment was for the want of pleasure and pain was the purpose of punishment. the purpose of punishment is to prevent a criminal from doing any further injury to the community and to prevent others from committing similar crimes

Cesare Beccaria was born on March 15, 1738, and died in 1794. Beccaria believed that punishment in the 1700s was barbaric, inhumane and unjust. He believed that each individual possessed free will and could choose whether or not to commit crimes, however, he also believed that they were easily manipulated.

Classical theory suggests that humans look out for themselves first, even if that means committing illegal or immoral acts, Beccaria stated that due to the need to look after the self-first offenders could be controlled and also predictable.

Beccaria stated that the purpose of the criminal justice system was to control deviant behaviour, to ensure that the punishment fits the crime; he also suggested that the aim of the just system should be that of deterrence rather than punishment. He was an advocate of the social contract, and breaches of that contract showed that the offender was aware of their actions and the consequences of breaching social responsibility. Beccaria advocated a fair and just punishment for breaching any social contracts.

In defining Beccaria and his theories, it can be stated that his views were that;

- Human behaviour as essentially rational
- Humans possessed the ability to choose right from wrong;
- They weigh up the consequences and then decide whether to commit the crime or not.
- A person's choice to breach the law was due to the desire to obtain pleasure and avoid pain.

Therefore, classical schools stated that any sentence that would be imposed should be enough to ensure that the pain of the sentence was severe enough to deter the behaviour.

Beccaria, (*who wrote; On Crimes and Punishment, in 1764 which started as a college essay*) believed that the general public was in favour of the social contract and that most were in favour of the abolishment of the death penalty. He also wrote that a person could be influenced in their decision making and influence those to commit crimes or not to. He was committed to the education of the population in the law and consequences of breaching them.

He was an advocate of the Social Contract. He believed that citizens would be happy to give up some of their freedoms "*so that (they) might enjoy the rest of it in peace and safety*".

Jeremy Bentham

Bentham was the forefather of Utilitarianism; this is the doctrine that the purpose of all actions should be to bring about the greatest happiness for the greatest number of people. He also coined the phrase Felicitous calculus, this is the is a moral calculus for estimating the probability that a person will engage in a particular kind of behaviour.

Jeremy Bentham was a British philosopher, born in 1748. Like Beccaria he believed that people have the ability to choose right from wrong. His explanation for criminal behaviour included the idea that people are basically hedonistic (seek pleasure), that is, they desire a high degree of pleasure and avoid pain. He wrote the now famous Introduction to the Principles of Morals and Legislation which was written in 1780.

He believed that he pain of punishment should be in excess to the please received by the crime. Bentham was also in favour of the prison system, and wrote extensively about prison design and management. He is also known for his invention of the idea of the "panopticon", (a circular prison with cells arranged around a central well, from which prisoners could at all times be observed)[4]..

Beccaria was the father of the concept of Utilitarianism; this is a principle that all actions should be to bring about the greatest happiness for the greatest number of people. He stated that punishment was a necessary

[4] https://en.wikipedia.org/wiki/Panopticon

evil but necessary it was, in order to stop even greater evils being committed on society.

Beccaria's and Bentham's theories argued that the proper objective of punishment should be to protect society and its laws. They both agreed that punishment should not be inflicted for revenge; instead, the primary purpose of punishment should be the reduction or deterrence of crime. In a nutshell: The Classical theory believed that the punishments inflicted should be just severe enough to outweigh any pleasures, to deter crime in future.

Neoclassical

> *Neoclassical theory used the classical theory but expanded it so that it also included the theory that there are certain factors, such as insanity which might inhibit the exercise of free will.*

This combination of the classical theory of free will, hedonistic pleasures seeking and responsibility of each individual, together with considerations of age, mental state and mitigating circumstances gave birth to what is often referred to as the Neoclassical Theory of Crime. This system was the foundation for the modern criminal justice systems which are now used in most countries in the world. Neoclassical theories of crime are rooted in the classical school.

- Places greater emphasis on rationality and cognition than classical criminologists

- **Examples:**
  - Rational choice theory
  - Routine activities theory

Cesare Lombroso

Lombroso was one of the first theorists who attempted to scientifically study criminal behaviour; he believed that physical stigmata, such as a long lower jaw, flattened nose, and long, apelike arms, identify a criminal. These biological characteristics were seen as atavism, or a throwback to earlier states in human evolution.

Lombroso in 1876 argued that the criminal is a separate species between modern and primitive humans physical shape of the head and face determined the "born criminal" - primitive and were unable to adapt to modern morality.

Cesare Lombroso and William Sheldon's interpretation of Criminals and examples of criminal types

Lombroso in 1876 argued that the criminal is a separate species between modern and primitive humans. He claimed that the physical shape of the head and face determined the "born criminal" - primitive and were unable to adapt to modern morality.

These people were primitive and were unable to adapt to modern morality. His view was based on genetics. The atavist (primitive genetic form) and had large jaws, high cheek bones, large ears, extra nipples, toes or fingers, and were insensitive to pain.

Thus, murderers were said to have:

- Cold, glassy, blood-shot eyes, curly, abundant hair, strong jaws, long ears and thin lips

Whilst sex offenders have:

- Glinting eyes, strong jaws, thick lips, lots of hair and projecting ears.'

Lombroso went further and suggested that from the surveys he had carried out in prison, he could detect physiological differences between different types of criminal.

His book, Criminal Man (1876), he claimed that nature vs. nurture was easily defined and he claimed that nature was the culprit in crime and not nurture.(*how you are brought up is irrelevant, it was your genes that decided*)

However, modern criminology can debunk this theory due to reseach and evidence showing how nurture (how they were brought up) can outweigh nature (predisposed from birth) in many criminals.

William Sheldon

[5]Sheldon was an American psychologist and numismatist. He was the creator of somatotype and constitutional psychology, this field attempted to correlate body types with behaviour, this included intelligence and social hierarchy.

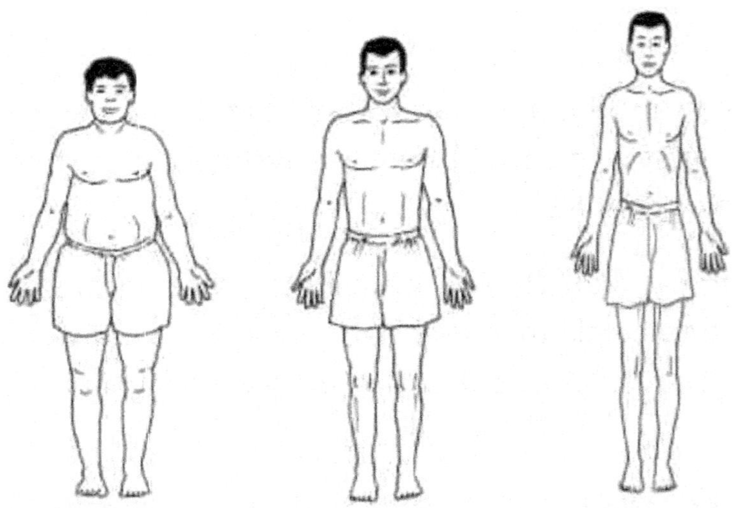

[5] Richard N. Walker (1978). "W. H. Sheldon" (PDF). Nature journal in Psychiatric

William Sheldon believed that people could be classified into three body shapes, which correspond with three different personality types.

- endomorphic (fat and soft) tend to be sociable and relaxed.
- ectomorphic (thin and fragile) are introverted and restrained
- mesomorphic (muscular and hard) tend to be aggressive and adventurous.

Sheldon, using a correlational study, found that many convicts were mesomorphic, and they were least likely to be ectomorphic (Sheldon et al 1949). This has since been attributed to the fact that mesomorphics were large and noticeable and therefore if seen at a scene of a crime they would be remembered easier.

The Positivist theory

> *Positive theorists primarily focused on biological and physiological factors of criminal behaviour. This school believed that criminals are born, and not made (Nature not Nurture), this school also advocated the XYY theory (abnormal chromosomes) and physical characteristics (size of jaw and teeth) determined a criminals path.*

The late 1800 saw the dawn of the positive school of thought or theory. This school of thought saw the beginning of the view that scientific research and investigation was vital to ensure that theories have basics and not theories based on ideas.

Positive school of thought sought to investigate the causes of crime, why it happened and what causes it. During this progressive and dynamic time interest and investigation into other sciences were growing, such as the natural sciences (physics, biology, chemistry etc.) were being developed.

Positive theorists believed that;

1. Human behavior is determined and not a matter of free will.
2. Criminals are fundamentally different from noncriminals.
3. Social scientists can be objective in their work.
4. Crime is frequently caused by multiple factors.

Ferri developed the field of criminal sociology and was the forefather of the positivist school of criminology; he outright denied that free will was an aspect of criminology.

A positive theorist who grew from the classical theory was Enrico Ferri who determined and claimed that a person's environment, the economy and society determined their criminality. He claimed that criminality could be defined by a person's';

a) Physical factors, including race, geographical location and climate

b) Anthropological factors such as age, sex, biological and physical condition

c) Social factors, i.e. economic conditions, religion and general customs

Ferri claimed that it was more important to prevent crime than to punish for it, he claimed that crime prevention was in the hands of the State, the State he claimed could reduce crime by provide social housing, parks and the ability to marry or divorce with freedom.

Ferri classified five types of offenders;

1. The born or instinctive criminal, who is a criminal from birth
2. The insane criminal, those affects by mental illnesses
3. The passional criminal, due to either emotional or mental illness
4. The occasional criminal, due to family background or family traits

5. The habitual criminal, an offender who from childhood or adulthood undertakes criminal behaviour and continues this from habit.

This was a very progressive theory in the 1800s. Positives did not believe in the classical theory of free will they believed that a person environment impact their behaviour, for instance, if a person has no food they will starve if they do not get food, (steal or die..!), therefore they will have no choice but to steal. Positive school of thought therefore stated that in order to reduce crime the state needed to ensure that the reasons for the crime must be reduced or eradicated.

Charles Darwin

The publication of Charles Darwin's theory of evolution in ***"On the Origin of Species"*** *in 1859 was the stepping stone which theorists such as Cesare Lombroso used in the formation of their theories of criminal behaviour. His views on the "born criminal" suggested that offenders were less evolved than non- criminals. His research established that it was possible to identify a criminal through their atavistic or apelike appearances and behaviours. The atavistic explanation has been disproven however, it established the process of scientific inquiry that characterised the positive school of criminology.*

Not a theorist of criminology, however I would just like to mention this progressive naturist and geologist, his theories that an animals development dependent on their environment and how the adaption or destruction of that environment impacted their behaviour.

Do you believe that the environmental factor is important in crime and criminality?

Locke John Locke (1632-1704)

Locke was more interested in an individual and their inalienable absolute rights than the social contract put forward by Hobbes, both philosophers worked in similar timeframes and although Locke agreed with some of Hobbes theories he believed that surrendering the right to self-govern in favour of the protection of sovereignty rules came with a social contract with provisions such as reciprocity,

> *'To understand political power aright, and derive it from its original, we must consider what state all men are naturally in, and that is a state of perfect freedom to order their actions and dispose of their possessions and persons as they think fit... A state also of equality, wherein all the power and jurisdiction is reciprocal, no one having more than another; there being nothing more evident than that creatures of the same species and rank... the use of the same faculties, should also be equal one amongst another without subordination or subjection...'*

Locke was an advent of power where power is necessary or that there should only be as much power as was need for the good of society. He stated that power should be given to the people who are elected by the people for the good of the people and not those whose power derives from hereditary powers or favour. *'And all this to be directed to no other end but the peace, safety, and public good of the people'* Locke spoke of the '*social contract*' with such knowledge and rigour it would have given the impression that this social contract was an actual event in history for which he has studied and become proficient and knowledgeable' .

His book was at the forefront of the Rule of Law, whereby fair procedure and the presumption of innocence. Becarria believed that laws could not be just and fair if the general public were not aware of them and the restrictions and sanctions clearly defined, that the law should not be retrospective (*guilty today for something you did yesterday which was legal at the time you did it*) and that the judiciary should not have the scope to interpret legislation unless in set rules. Furthermore he believed that punishment should be a deterrent to the general public not just the individual involved and also that morals have no place in sentencing for legal breaches.

> **Rule of law.** 'It is better for the law to rule than one of its citizens' ~Aristotle *(however it is vital that that ruling law to be ruled lawfully also)*

Article 40.1 of the Irish Constitution states:

All citizens shall, as human persons, be held equal before the law. This shall not be held to mean that the State shall not in its enactments have due regard to differences of capacity, physical and moral, and of social function.

The rule of law, was popularised by AV Dicey in 1885, the Rule of law implies absolute supremacy of law. It guarantees that an individual can ascertain with reasonable certainty what legal powers are available to the government if an individual's rights are infringed, as stated in

> ***Article 40.4.1***, no citizen shall be deprived of his personal liberty save in accordance with law,

It does not exempt the officials and others from the duty of obedience to the law which governs other citizens or from jurisdiction of ordinary tribunals. However, this is now subject to the Supremacy of EU law.

Rousseau Jean-Jacques Rousseau (1712-1778)

Unlike Locke, Rousseau believed in the theory of the "*social contract*" however he further defined this as more in terms of '*social order'* than the 'social contract'. Rousseau believed that man is inherently good. *'Man is born innocent and good, free and equal, but the corrupting powers of civilisation are responsible for the evil situation in which he finds himself'*. This belief in the inherent good of man was defined further when Rousseau stated that the inherent goodness of man was corrupted by the past and past events. However he believed that this still held man in chains due to being held to a higher order in the social contract. He also believed that the people reigned supreme and no sovereign can remove that right he also believed that society thrives when the masses are happy.

> *'and in which each, while uniting himself with all, may still obey himself alone, and remain as free as before'.*

The theory Rousseau put forward was that the general population and well as the individual are under the power of the "*general will*'. He stated that people will obey when forced to obey, he stated that society did well under this guise, however he believed that societies thrived when the force to obey was less prevalent, however this theory has been debunked by modern philosophers. [6]. Rousseau recognises that self-preservation is only one principle of motivation for the actions of humans or what differentials humans from animals he stated was the human soul and the ability to empathise and feel guilt or pity.

---

[6] LOCKE AND ROUSSEAU:. Jamie Gianoutsos. http://www.baylor.edu/content/services/document.php?id=37670

This is *"an innate repugnance to see his fellow suffer*"." And the other difference between humans and animals is that humans are *"if acting legally and within the laws of the land*" free agents to come and go as they please and have the ability to reason any situation which they may find themselves part of.

Chapter three

Modern Theories of Criminology

Modern theories of crime vary from

- Crime is part of human nature.

to

- Crime is based on biological, psychological, sociological, and/or economic aspects.

Modern criminology has taken the works of its predecessors and built on them, the development of modern criminology can be attributed to theorists such as Durkheim, Sutherland and Merton's, the modern theories are;

- Anomie or Strain Theory
- Social Learning Theory
- Social Control Theory
- Labelling Theory
- Radical Theory
- Deterrence Theory
- An Economic Model of Crime

Anomie or Strain Theory

- *This school believes that people commit crimes when they see no legitimate way to achieve their goals. This theory may explain why there is more crime among the economically disadvantaged. Theorists believed that crime was as a direct result of lower class frustration and anger. According to strain theory, people feel strain when they are exposed to cultural goals that they are unable to obtain because they do not have access to culturally approved means of achieving those goals*

Robert Merton in 1938 wrote about a major contradiction in the U.S. between cultural goals and social structure. He called the contradiction anomie. For Merton, the contradiction between the cultural goal of achieving wealth and the social structure's inability to provide legitimate institutional means for achieving the goal. [7] (Merton. P, 1938)

Society defines success in terms of certain goals, but does not always provide the means or opportunity for people to reach these goals. Merton argued that the limited availability of legitimate institutionalized means to wealth puts a strain on people. People adapt through:

- Conformity—playing the game, achieve goals by legitimate means
- Innovation—pursuing wealth by illegitimate means and finding ways to achieve.
- Ritualism—not actively pursuing wealth but dreaming about it.

---

[7] Merton. P, 1938; "Science, Technology and Society in Seventeenth Century England", Osiris, Vol. IV, pt. 2, pp. 360-632. Bruges: St. Catherine Press, 1938

- Retreatism—dropping out, not even trying.
- Rebellion—rejecting the goal of wealth and the institutional means of getting it and creating a new system.

Merton also argued that individuals perceptions of economic and social inequality lead to feelings of envy, mistrust, and aggression, this leads to

Lower classes feel both deprived and embittered and in turn turn to crime to reduce the feelings of inequality.

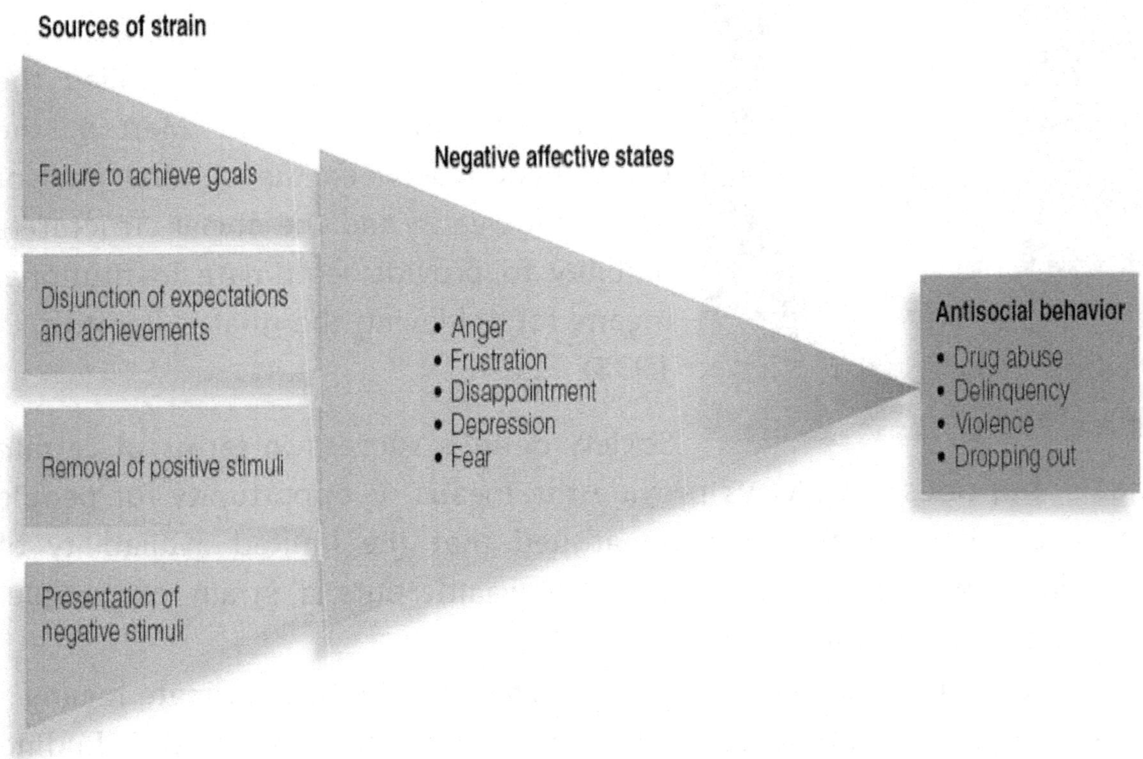

Social Learning Theory

Edwin H. Sutherland—in his theory of differential association—was the first 20th-century criminologist to argue that criminal behaviour was learned.

This theory, modified, remains one of the most influential theories of crime causation. Sutherland's theory that persons who become criminal do so because of contacts with criminal patterns and isolation from anti-criminal patterns

Warr and Stafford (1991:862) studied the mechanism by which delinquency is socially transmitted. They compared the effect of peer's attitude and effect of peer's behaviour and found that delinquency stemmed rather from behaviour of peers than the consequence of attitudes acquired from peers. This means that Sutherland's assertion that attitude of peers is major factor of delinquency is incomplete. The attitudes of adolescents indeed do influent delinquency. "However, quite apart from the attitudes of adolescents and those of their friends, the behaviour of friends has a strong, independent effect on adolescents' behaviour."[8]

[8] Mark Warr, Mark Stafford(1991). The influence of delinquent peers: What they think or what they do?. Criminology.

Social Control Theory

> *Social control depends on people's anticipating the consequences of their behavior; people who believe they have little to lose are more likely to become deviant*

Sutherland's theory that persons who become criminal do so because of contacts with criminal patterns and isolation from anti-criminal patterns. The most detailed elaboration of modern social control theory is attributed to Travis Hirsch who wrote the 1969 book, *Causes of Delinquency.*[9](Hirschi. T, 1969). Hirsch argued that delinquency should be expected if a juvenile is not properly socialized by establishing a strong bond to society, consisting of:

- Attachment to others, strong social attachments encourage conformity and lesson criminal behaviours.
- Opportunity, the greater a person's access to legitimate opportunity, the greater the advantages of conformity
- Involvement in conventional activities, extensive involvement in legitimate activities inhibits deviance.
- Belief in the moral order and law, strong belief in conventional morality and respect for authority figures restrain tendencies toward deviance.

---

[9] Travis Hirschi 1969; University of California Press,

Labelling Theory

> *Labeling theory suggests that people defined themselves as society sees them, labelling can start in childhood, the labels can go from they're a good kid, just a bit wild, and progress to they're a bad apple they are. Therefore, crime is not always defined by the behavior of criminals, but to societies reaction to it.(reread my own statement in the beginning, of socially acceptable criminal behaviours)*

Labelling can go from the community to the criminal justice system, criminals rarely see themselves as criminals, they often state things like, they had it coming, r they have insurance.

The labeling theory argues that once a person commits a first criminal act and gets processed in the system, they are labeled negatively as a criminal.

- The label becomes a self-fulfilling prophecy.

Labelling theory suggests that people in power decide what acts are crimes, and the act of labelling someone a criminal is what makes him a criminal. Once a person is labelled a criminal, society takes away his opportunities, which may ultimately lead to more criminal behaviour.

Once a criminal is convicted or incarcerated it is difficult to remove that label, society labels them and getting a job can prove difficult, leading them straight back into crime due to necessity or vengeance.

If you refer back to race and ethnicity you can see for example, young travellers being labelled as "trouble" etc, this label then defines all travellers behaviour as deviant, this furthers the social isolation and labelling and creating a vicious circle, if I am trouble then I'll be trouble and so it goes on.

Radical Theory

Radical theories argue that capitalism requires people to compete against each other in the pursuit of material wealth.

The more unevenly wealth is distributed; the more likely people are to find persons weaker than themselves that they can take advantage of in their pursuit of wealth. Theories of crime causation that are generally based on a Marxist theory of class struggle.

Radical Theorists believe that;

a. Society is seen to "function" in terms of the general interests of a ruling class rather than "everyone".

b. The potential for class conflict is always present - a ruling class has to continually act to reproduce its domination of other classes in society.

For instance, there is a belief amongst some racial theory camp that class structure produces social control, such instances can be explained, for instance, social welfare, this is a payment to those who cannot afford the cost of living and who are either unemployed or disabled etc, radical theorists claim this is a form of social control, keeping the lower classes poor with institutionalism and over reliance on the ruling classes for their means, the ruling class in return abusing this by making rules that benefit the ruling classes while dressing it up to appear like “they are being supported and helped”

Some theorists of criminology believe that only when capitalism is replaced by socialism, will there be a solution to the crime problem.

Deterrence Theory

This theory is advocates that an individual chooses to commit a crime, but this choice is influence by the fear of punishment. Unlike choice theory which states that a person will weigh up the choices before deciding on the criminal behaviour, deterrence on the other hand emphasises that people will not commit a crime if the punishment outweigh the pleasure, or that "it's just not worth it", in essence stopping the criminal act before its even taken place by ensuring that any offenders are aware of the punishment and any sanctions which will be imposed.

This punishment must be severe enough to prevent the offender from partaking in it in the first place. (This sounds familiar, Neo-classical..!) However, some offenders are still of the thought that should they get caught some police officers will not pursue a conviction due to the relatively minor offence.

In order for punishment to be deterrence then justice must not only be done, it must be seen to be done. However, research has shown that simply increasing police presence or extending sentences for offences has not brought crime down.

An Economic Model of Crime

An economic model of crime claims that a person will make the same decision when faced with the same consequences, for instance if the reward is the same as the last offence then they will commit again, if they find and easy target they will strike again, this is why some offenders will return to burgle the same house a number of times, this could be due to the fact that the house is easy to access with an easy target and easy goods to sell, and also may be down to the fact that the victim may replace the stolen items quickly with more good quality and easy to offload goods making it attractive, if they can commit a crime knowing the rewards and costs in advance they will probably follow the same course of action.

Deterrence and Econometrics

The justice model stresses or the just deserts model advocates that if an offender breaks the law they should get punished,

Utilitarian punishment philosophy is based on the theory that punishment is a necessary evil. It is both protection and deterrence.

The economic model of crime stresses that criminal behaviour follows a calculation whereby the criminal explores the perceived costs, rewards, and risks of alternative actions.

Deterrence aims to ensure that victims are not soft targets, and that the general public should ensure that rewards of crime are reduced by;

- Concealing goods
- Removing goods from public sight
- Identifying property with markings

Environmentalism

Theorist claim that offenders are more likely to offend in an area they know well, this increases their chances of escape and evade capture.

Research suggests that burglars will commit crimes in areas they know well and times they know that there is less likelihood of getting caught, this means that some areas were high target areas with high instances of burglary in specific areas.

Ethnicity and Crime

Each individual Country has specific ethnic groups which are far more likely involved with the criminal justice system than others. The ethnic groups which have this elevated status can vary from Country to Country and Continent to Continent. Ireland does not have much empirical or statistics results on other ethnicities as of yet as research in this area is not commonplace, however, there is some research regarding travellers, their race is white Irish, their ethnicity is traveller, (*although not defined by the state as ethnic*) but defined by ***Sinead Ni Shuinear (1994, 2002)*** argues, after Barth, that Travellers are definitely an ethnic group:[10]

- They are biologically self-reproducing (Travellers marry Travellers, you cannot become a Traveller)
- They share fundamental cultural values They make up a boundaried social group in terms of communication (their own language, Cant or Gammon
- They identify themselves (as Travellers)
-

Therefore some attention will be paid to this ethnic group before taking International statistics into consideration. Firstly, Traveller men are between five and 11 times more likely than other men to be imprisoned, while Traveller women face a risk of imprisonment as much as 18 to 22 times higher than that of the general population.[11] It is clear that in proportion to male travellers, female travels are at a higher risk of being sentenced to a prison sentence. The majority of sentenced being meted to travellers are for theft and property offences. Travellers are 11 times

---

[10] This definition is not as yet been accepted by the establishment

[11] The Irish Penal Reform Trust. Travellers in the Irish Prison System

more likely to be stopped and questioned by the Gardaí than a settled person and the unemployment rate for travellers aged 15-24 is over 70%.

In the UK suggests that black people whose families originate from the Caribbean in the 1940s are more likely to be criminalised[12], also figures from recent statistics in the UK state that Asians are 11 times more likely to be stopped and questioned at the borders, while Asians were twice as likely to be stopped and searched than white counterparts. While black people are 6 times more likely to be stopped and searched than their white counterparts[13] and 6 times more likely to be arrested than white people. The varying reasons for the higher numbers of black Asian and travellers being arrested, charged or jailed for offences may be explained by the fact that these ethnic groups high a higher proportion of younger males and females than the white population and crime peaks between ages of 21 and 24 meaning there are simply more younger people in these ethnic groups than white accounting for the higher rates. (This is debatable, just has statistical backing). (Povis and Walmsley (2002)).

There appears to be a variety of factors which are responsible for the variations and higher crime and sentencing rates. Travellers have a much lower school finishing rate than settled people and some Asian and black groups have this low levels of education which can place them at a higher risk of offending means that they are less able to achieve their goals through legitimate means and are likely to experience one or more factors that put them at risk of offending.' However this explanation places the emphasis on the ethnicity and not the individual offender. This may even suggest that offenders are victims of institutionalised racism.

---

[12] Hiro, Dilip. Black British, White British: A History of Race Relations in Britain. London:Paladin, 1992

[13] A press release from the Home Office Press (11 July 2006) entitled 'Criminal Justice System tackling Racism and Racist Crime'

Feminist theory

> *Feminist criminology emphasizes gender issues and seeks to develop appreciation of the role of women in the causes of crime, victimisation of women in the criminal justice system, and the control of crime.*

Feminists see women and girls are doubly affected by theories and crime, Feminist theories of crime ask questions such as

- Do traditional male-cantered theories of crime apply to women?"
- What explains the universal fact that women are far less likely than men to involve themselves in criminal activity?

It wasn't until the 1970 that this school of criminology was born, this was due to the perceived rise in criminality by women, the feminist theory of criminality worked on the premise that female committed crimes for different reasons than men, it was also a feminist theory that the criminal justice system was patriarchal and crime was defined by men for men and women were not catered for either in criminality or punishment.

Lombroso (above) believed that women who committed crime were doubly deviant; they even went so far as to describe female criminals as looking physically like men and normal women were not criminally inclined. In the 1970s Dr Klein set out to debunk these theories and determined that female criminality was in part due to economic needs rather than deviancy. In Ireland in 2015 only 3.5% of the prison population were female; this insight shows the levels of female offenders showing the gender gap interred.

Types of feminism

- Liberal Feminism: Gender differences in crime rates traced to gender differences in socialization
- Marxist Feminism: Women forced to commit crime to survive in capitalist society
- Radical Feminism: Patriarchy precedes capitalism; gender more important than class
- Socialist Feminism: Sees capitalism and patriarchy as equally important
- Multicultural Feminism: Stresses importance of race and ethnicity along with gender and class[14]

Feminist theories of crime suggest that tradition theories of crime do not apply to females, to date there is little empirical evidence or data specifically for female criminality, however, the limited research does show that the geographical, social and economic backgrounds of female offenders are similar to their male counterparts. Feminist criminology focuses on trying to recognise female offending from the feminist point of view, which believes that women are faced with special circumstances living in a patriarchal society

Modern feminist theories of criminology

Research in the 1990s has divided opinion with its theories lying with social theories of crime, that women commit crimes because of social needs and not because of any natural predisposition. Research in this area is still on-going with emphasis on gender bias and disparity in sentencing rather than female criminalities causes.

[14] Steve E. Barkan. 2015. Criminology: A Sociological Understanding, Prentice Hall

Age and Crime

Age has long been a major factor in criminal behaviour, as is the notion that criminality reduces with age. Criminal age peaks in the mid-20s, with the highest instances of criminal behaviour in youths age 18 to 24.

The explanations for the peak stem from age, stamina, agility, speed to aggression. Teenagers have few connections to traditional adult institutions, such as work and family.[15] Teens are tempted by the quick money and rewards such as power or status and the pleasure seeking adrenaline and sensual pleasures. Teens and young adults have no responsibility and are supported by their carer's, and therefore have no reasoning as to the consequences of their actions, especially financial consequences, "*if they commit crime, they will not be expected to pay their fines, their parents are expected to*". Deviance in teenage years is often defined or described as the teen "*just growing up*"[16] As teens progress into adulthood after the peak age of 24 changes are prominent in their lives, this is when many "grow up", there have been 6 changes identified as important in the decline in criminal behaviour after the peak age and adulthood assumed from 25 years on.[17]

1. People have better access to legitimate sources of material goods and excitement: jobs, home, alcohol and sex.
2. People are "expected to grow up" and increase their responsibility, deviance is no longer acceptable and maturity is expected from society around them.

---

[15] Warr, Mark. (1998) "Life-Course Transitions and Desistance from Crime." *Criminology*
[16] Jolin, Annette, and Gibbons, Don. (1987) "Age Patterns in Criminal Involvement." *International Journal of Offender Therapy and Comparative Criminology*
[17] Steffensmeier, Darrell; Allan, Emilie; Harer, MILES; and Streifel, Cathy. (1989)"Age and the Distribution of Crime." *American Journal of Sociology*

3. People don't "hang out" with their friends as much when they get older, friendship is replaced with relationships and assumed responsibility

4. Legally and socially responsible for deviant behaviour.

5. As people get older the types of crimes may also change, fraud and gambling increase due to the fact that they is an assumption that there is less risk and more return in these crimes.

6. As a person gets older they analyse and become more aware of their actions and the consequences, this leads to a decline in the self and self wants. The meaning of life is questioned more and how their actions affect others.

The trends seem to increase in urban and populated areas; this is in part due to access to the items of their desire. Peer pressure is another cause, other friends daring and betting they won't commit crimes, or gang affiliation or "belonging" requires deviance and criminal activity as a prerequisite to joining. Until the peak at 25 there is very little in the crime rates and deviancy in females and males (excluding prostitution which a dominantly female profession).

The most common finding across countries, groups, and historical eras is that crime tends to be a young persons' game.

Routine Activities Theory

> *This new perspective within the modern schools of criminological believed that the contributions of routine activities theory and situational crime prevention, as well as the ecological approaches contribute to criminal behaviour or lack of it.*

Routine activities theory is a theory that criminals balance the pros and cons of committing crimes.

Routine activities theory extends the classical approach. It however does go deeper in definition. Routine activities theory claims that criminals balance the pros and cons long before they commit the crime and only commit it when they have weighed all sides.

Routine activities theorists claim that

- self-interest motivates criminal offenders to commit criminal acts;
- many individuals may be motivated to break laws.

The better the reward the more pleasure is derived from it, such as car theft and joyriding; these crimes give positive rewards for negative behaviour and may induce a person to commit a crime.

Protection does lesson crimes, CCTV, gates security guards, this is due to the fact that the cost to the offender is higher in terms of time and effort and therefore lessening the attractiveness of the target or victim.

*(**Example**; Crime is likely to occur when a motivated offender and a suitable target come together in absence of a capable guardian.)*

Mental Disorder and Crime

According to ***Section 3 of the Mental Health Act,*** *defines mental illness, severe dementia or significant intellectual disability where—*

(a) because of the illness, disability or dementia, there is a serious likelihood of the person concerned causing immediate and serious harm to himself or herself or to other persons, or

(b) (i) because of the severity of the illness, disability or dementia, the judgment of the person concerned is so impaired that failure to admit the person to an approved centre would be likely to lead to a serious deterioration in his or her condition or would prevent the administration of appropriate treatment that could be given only by such admission, and

(ii) the reception, detention and treatment of the person concerned in an approved centre would be likely to benefit or alleviate the condition of that person to a material extent.

The medical definition of mental illness is different, it is defined as "a mental disorder is considered to be a group of clinically significant behaviours or patterns that cannot be an expectable response to a particular event or situation and must be considered a manifestation of a behavioural, psychological, or biological dysfunction in the person".

Police and Gardai are poorly equipped to deal with offenders with mental health issues and this can result in unintentional abuse of positions and also necessary treatment and sentencing are not being identified and recognised. There are calls for more training in real life situations for the gardai, this is essential for empathy understanding and experience. Mental illness can result in heartbreak when crime results and there is not enough training, such as the Abbeylara shooting in which a member of the gardai shot and killed a mentally ill man, this resulted in much more training for gardai in recognising and responding to mentally ill criminal behaviour. Dealing with mental illness is now more hands on, doctors, family and trained medial staff can deal with mentally ill offender and those at risk of offending. The types of offences which people with mental illness tend to partake in and come before the courts are but not limited to; criminal damage burglary, public order offences handling stolen goods shoplifting, fraud, and dishonestly.[18] The instances of abuse and public order offences rise when the mental illness is coupled with substance abuse.

Many offenders with mental illness feel that the criminal justice system punishes them for being themselves, having an illness which is "them". Many offenders with mental illnesses are involuntarily committed and given treatment, there are of course those who agree to being committed and treated, but where the offender refuses then commitment at the central mental hospital may be ordered. This in part is society's need that justice needs to be seen to be done. It is vital going forward that possible offenders who have mental illnesses need to be identified much faster than they already are, to recognise the offences before they are committed because of the behaviours of the mentally ill person.

Mentally ill offenders can be treated in specialised hospitals or in prisons, depending on the severity of the mental illness and the tools available in prisons. Unfortunately there are still mentally ill offenders who are not diagnosed at all, either prior to their incarceration, or during their stay, leaving them unprepared for the release and destined to repeat their offending. Raising awareness of mental illness is vital for all those in and outside of the criminal justice system, removing the stigma of mental illness so those affected by mental illness are more likely to come forward to seek treatment.

---

[18] (Bean, 2009).

Rawls' John Bordley Rawls (1921 - 2002)

Rawls' theory is based upon three elements: a vision of society as it ought to be; a view of moral theory and its significance; and the derivation of principles which will enable an expression of that vision to be enunciated so as to reflect moral theory. (Curzon, 1995)

Rawl attempted to define social justice in the context of a social contract; he uses the theory of original position to define the ideal social order. The perception of justice for Rawls starts with "justice as fairness". This is based on the original moral theory of utilitarianism (although I am not convinced of this being utilitarian, but Rawlsonian "*his own moral theory*").

Original position

The hypothetical society which was chosen under Rawls "original position" revolved around a congress who objectivity discussed and decided in a set of fundamental principles which were at the forefront of their society. This society would be governed on the principles of what are objectively "just" (not one individual persons interpretation of just but that of the whole society)

This theory is based on the presumption that people and societies consent to being governed. He claimed that:

"the basic structure of society, or more exactly, the way in which the major social institutions distribute fundamental rights and duties and determine the division of advantages from social cooperation. By major institutions I understand the political constitution and the principal economic and social arrangements".

Rawl committed a lot of his research to the theories of social organisation, the social organisation theory would suggest that people are not free to choose or to make rational choices or make just decisions and inherently civil disobedience will result in punishments. (See Also: Rawls - the veil of Ignorance course notes), this society will only exist where there is fair treatment of every individual.

Rawl however led this theory from a utopian point of view, whereby everyone will do good if they are taken care within society, the good of the greater over the good of the few...he stated that: *"everyone is presumed to act justly and to do his part in upholding just institutions".* (Surely then this means that Rawls new society would have to be subjected to compliance?)

The veil of ignorance

In order for fairness and impartiality in society it is according to Rawls imperative that all bias is removed. For instance, all bias towards the rich or poor and religious or non-religious, advantaged or disadvantaged need to be removed before we can see impartial procedures. The principle of the veil of ignorance is significant insofar as it removed any personal perception of what good is, it is the good of society as a general rule than any individual.

This principle of the veil of ignorance ensures consistency and fairness in the division of wealth, food, social and religion; therefore the theories of the social contract emerge. The Social contract consists of: [19]

- the original position with representatives

[19] my own interpretation.

- the two principles of justice structured by the basic principle of fair and just
- the actual society with no bias towards any persons with *'fairness is justice'* at its core.

The representatives of this new social order must be in the original position, this is to ensure that there is a free, just and fair social order. The original order is based on each and every person and representative not knowing their social order when determining the rules of fair and just, for instance, the persons or representatives would not know if they were a lowly servant or royalty, they would have no idea of social standing or financial status or their religious affiliation when they are defining this new social structure.[20]

<u>The Veil of Ignorance</u>. The representatives do not know anything about the persons they represent: their sex, race, physical handicaps, social class, or conception of the good. It is imperative that the representatives are aware of psychology and sociology, for instance, that humans remember the past, anticipate the future, and also socialise and interact in the present, they are of all abilities and partake in all types of social interactions, finally they know that there are those in this original position who are sick or disabled

[20] John Rawls. A THEORY OF JUSTICE.
http://www2.econ.iastate.edu/classes/econ362/hallam/readings/rawl_justice.pdf

Two principles of justice

These two types of the principles of justice:

- **political justice**: rights of the many outweigh the rights of the few.
- **social justice**: each person is to have an equal right to basic liberties and social and economic inequalities are in the favour of the least advantaged and that all representative positions which are available will be available to all within society regardless of their financial, religious or social standing.[21] This principle also explains that any inequalities should be in everyone's benefit.

Rawls' theory requests the representatives to conceive of society *"as a fair system of cooperation over time, from one generation to the next"* and also *"a structure of basic institutions we enter only by birth and exit only by death";* [22]

The theoretical society will then see its citizens free and equal, these citizens will have *"a capacity for a sense of justice and for a conception of the good."* Which will result in *"fully cooperating members of society,"* [23] *"...to act in relation to others on terms that they also can publicly endorse"*

Rawls rejects Utilitarianism in the original position and the veil of ignorance due to the inability to give individual rights and freedoms and that this principle works against the original position, he further states that utility blurs the lines between individual and society misleadingly *"conflat[es] all persons into one," revealing that "Utilitarianism does not take seriously the distinction between persons"* also defines

[21] John Rawls, A Theory of Justice, page 302

[22] John Rawls, A Theory of Justice. Cambridge, Mass., 1971, page 152.

[23] John Rawls, Political Liberalism, New York, NY: Columbia University Press, 1993.

"Utilitarianism as the principle of utility . (What's best for the wellbeing of society). . it hold for all kinds of subjects ranging from the conduct of individuals to the organization of society as a whole as well as to the law of peoples."[24]

[24] John Rawls, Political Liberalism, New York, NY: Columbia University Press, 1993. Page 13

Rawls Reasonable Citizens

Rawl refers to the reasonable citizens. Reasonable citizens *"are ready to propose principles and standards as fair terms of cooperation,* these citizens then *abide by them willingly, given the assurance that others will likewise do so*[25]. Likewise, *"requires that when those terms are proposed as the most reasonable terms of fair cooperation, those proposing them must... think it at least reasonable for others to accept them, as free and equal citizens, and not as dominated or manipulated... under the pressure of an inferior political or social position."*[26]

Rawls also recognise in the reasonable citizen those "willing to bear the consequences of the burdens of judgment." [27] in this explanation Rawls recognises that people can and do disagree on subjects and topics, this however does not have to become a biased interpretation of the other persons judgement. Rawls defined the following such sources of disagreement or burdens of judgment as:

- Different types of evidence,
- How different people see different situations,
- Principles and rules not being defined clearly,
- The diversity of human beings and their interpretation of ideals
- Two different parties have completely opposite definition of the same principle
- Some institution requiring citizens to choose one belief over another

Going back to the original position, the representatives of the ideal society under which Rawls theory of the veil of ignorance falls are given

---

[25] John Rawls, A Theory of Justice. Cambridge, Mass., 1971

[26] Rawls, J. 1993In The Law of Peoples (1999) page 49

[27] Rawls, J. 1993In The Law of Peoples (1999) page 58

the task of selecting principles of justice that will govern the basic structure of society.

To show briefly how they will reason, let us consider whether they would choose a principle of equal opportunity, say, a principle that would make economic discrimination on the basis of race, gender, or religion unjust.

One of the ways in which the representatives can achieve this original position within the veil of ignorance is to remove any kids of discrimination, such as race, religion, gender or colour. Ruling out discrimination will ensure that all citizens regardless of their race, religion, gender or colour will be afforded equal opportunities.

However, Rawls was aware that some person within society must be given more resources, power and income than other to balance the books, to pay bills or manage workers; Rawls suggest that this power can be allowed under the strictest conditions are met, such as:

(a) the project will make life better off for the people who are now worst off, for example, by raising the living standards of everyone in the community and empowering the least advantaged persons to the extent consistent with their well-being,

(b) access to the privileged positions is not blocked by discrimination according to irrelevant criteria.

Rawls principle of Justice

Rawls defined "justice as fairness". These principles stem from the following principles:

1. Each individual is entitled equal basic liberties, freedom and liberty, the same liberty and freedom enjoyed by everyone else.
2. If there are social inequalities within the citizens then then inequalities should be addressed insofar as all opportunities are available to everyone regardless of their social background. And those are least privileged get more chances than those who are privileged.

Rawls definition of the "fully adequate scheme of equal basic liberties." These basic liberties included:

1. freedom of thought
2. liberty of conscience "liberty as applied to religious, philosophical, and moral view of our relation to the world."
3. political liberties "freedom of speech and the press, and freedom of assembly"
4. freedom of association
5. freedoms specified by the liberty and integrity of the person "freedom from slavery and serfdom and freedom of movement and choice regarding occupation"
6. rights and liberties covered by the rule of law

Rawls therefore requires the representative in the original position to ensure basic equal liberties for all citizens. To make a *"rationally prudential choice"* regarding their social contract, ensuring that all social and economic positions are to everyone's advantage, and open to all. These representatives were to use reasoning and the veil of ignorance (not knowing their special positon within this new society) when deciding on a stable and democratic society. This new concept ensures basic personal liberties and freedoms *"when it includes conceptions of what is of value in human life, as well as ideals of personal*

The Chicago School and the US theories

> *The Chicago school claims that society, in the form of the community, wields a major influence on human behaviour.*

It must be noted that criminological and theories of criminal behaviours developed differently in Europe and the USA. This school of thought started with "Criminality and Economic Conditions". Bonger's (1916)

In the 1900s the USA saw the growth from a rural farming landscape to an industrial city or urban landscape which was seen in 1700/1800s Britain and Europe, with it came poverty and crime similar to that seen in Europe, causes such as low pay, horrific working conditions coupled with slum housing and poor conditions gave birth to crime and poverty, the USA did not deal with the woes of city living like Europe as they had come to this growth over 100 years later so the Chicago school was born to deal with a similar problem at a different time and continent.

However, the policing and policing policies which were born in the UK were used in the USA, these policies survived the revolution and even after the revolution many of the UKs policing policies were continued, the Chicago model used the Chicago theories of crime coupled with the UKs policing policies, it can be defined as a type of hybrid crime and policing policy which was the forerunner to the modern USA crime and policing policies.

Robert Park and Ernest Burgess

This also builds on the routine activities theory, the defensible spaces theory suggests that routine activity places may be regulated far more easily than the routine activities of persons, in criminology this theory suggests that places are easier to watch than people.

The research carried out by Park and Burgess involved detailed statistics and geographic maps, they researched the relationship between crime and selected urban social variables, the variable which they started with were poverty, overcrowding and dilapidation. Further research by Shaw in 1927 found environmental association between crime and delinquency He framed the term or label, delinquency Shaw found that areas with more slums such as fringe districts where overcrowding was rife suffered with more crime, he also stated that districts or slums with high population of foreign and black residents who were poorly or unskilled workers suffered from a higher rate of crime. This research was also carried out in Boston and Philadelphia by Shaw and McKay in 1942 also showed higher rates of crime where there was a high instance of population transition supported the claims of Park and Burgess that crime and delinquency producing social disorganisation.

Not based on the Chicago School but building on it Oscar Newman conducted research in 1972 which he claimed crime that a defensible space was a more rational theory, he claimed that if there was no way of the residents of an area to supervise the area they lived then crime would go unnoticed per se, i.e. high rise towers were no supervisory and only the people on any given floor could know what was going on in that area. Leaving for a scope for unsupervised criminal behaviour in the other areas of the block. He changed his theories in the 1980s however, due to widespread criticism of his research and findings.

The Chicago coined the term deprivation, this terms defines deprivation as being by researching the following:

- the basis of unemployment,
- children in low learning households,
- overcrowding, households lacking basic amenities,
- lack of cars,
- low educational attainment,
- mortality rates as a health measure,

Further research in the UK by the Social Exclusion Unit has said that a study of 20 of the most deprived estates in the UK found that 23 per cent of schools which were specifically for estates achieved no GCSEs at grades A to C, a significantly higher "failure" rate, also residents of estates were over ten times more likely to be the victims of crime.

Right Realism

Yet another school of thought, this school believed that crime was within the individual and not society as a whole, Right Realists saw crime as a result of the combination of a person's genetic makeup and their social environment. They claimed that because of a person's genetic predisposition some people would be inclined to engage in criminality. They argued that this predisposition could be controlled through social conditioning in the family, in the school and other community activities. While it was suggested that lower class families and lone parents were the most likely to be involved in criminal activity, this did not explain white collar crime and therefore falters in its findings.

Right realists claimed that there needed to be tougher laws which should be enforced to the maximum, Right realists believed that crime was not due to a social structure but where social discipline was not used.

This school of thought has not been without its critics, the main criticisms include but not limited to the following;

- Crime is not limited to the streets, there are far more factors at play
- No accounting for white collar crime in their findings
- Focuses on individualistic crimes and not crimes to society or invisible crimes (insurance fraud etc)

Left idealists

Left idealists were in complete contrast to the right realists, they believed that the capitalists or high power individuals in society were responsible for the majority of the worst crimes within society (*because the poor wanted what the rich had and it was their fault when the poor rebelled and tried to obtain those things*). They had the opinion and beliefs that lower class individuals only committed crimes in retaliation against oppression from the elite. They had no wish to determine the causes of crime, they just wanted someone to blame.

They did not focus on the crimes themselves, they were more interested in blame, however, this school faltered in their theories, the questions the left idealist theorists were asked the following questions in order to explain their theories;

- Which high power individuals within society were responsible for the burglaries and home invasions by default, the idealists believed this was rebelling against oppression.
- Explain why middle or lower class individuals were more like to attack other middle or lower class individuals, where were the high power individuals in this or why was it their fault.
- If the elite were responsible for the lower class crime then how could the idealists explain, rape, domestic abuse, in terms of a rebellions against the elite

White Collar Crime

Edwin Sutherland first coined the phrase "white collar crime" in the 1940s; this was to define crimes committed by so called, respectable people. This was to describe crimes which had they been committed by other offenders at this time, would have been classed as criminal and probably charged also. This was the beginning of criminalising behaviour of those in power and positions of power when partaking in criminal behaviour, such behaviour as; Insider dealing, money laundering, credit card fraud, insurance fraud, time share and pension fraud.

Insider Dealing

Insider dealing is a criminal offence; it is capable of a criminal sanction of up to 10 years in prison, and a fine of up to €10million euro.

Insider dealing can be defined as occurring when a person or parties have price sensitive information which is not generally available about a company's performance and deals in that information to make a profit.

1. Member of admin, management, board etc.
2. Holds capital.
3. Has access to the information,
4. criminal activities.

IFCMP Act 2009 and the Market Abuse (Directive) Regulations 2005 defines information as precise and sensitive, it is not freely available information and it relates to the shares etc. this information is not yet public and an investor would use in their decision to invest or information that could affect the prices of the securities.

Civil courts may direct the dealer (the person taking and using the information) to pay compensation to anyone who was not in information and lost money due to that.

Money laundering

Money laundering is a process whereby the proceeds of criminal means are concealed (drug trafficking, gun smuggling, corruption, etc.) and given the appearance of coming from legitimate sources. This is done giving the illegal money the appearance of legitimacy and inserting it into the economy by.

1. Concealing or disguising the true nature of the property.
2. Converting, transferring, handling, acquiring, possessing or using the property; or
3. Removing the property from, or bringing the property into, the State.

The advent of the offshore bank accounts and Swiss bank accounts which were not only a tax haven but also free from patrolling by the Police helped to distinguish the source of the proceeds. One of the more famous havens was the Cayman Islands

Money laundering is an increasing concern for all Governments, especially because of its links to terrorism. It is vital that all countries sign up to combat money laundering, this international cooperation between police and financial agencies can go somewhat towards the fight against money laundering and terrorist financing.

Under ***Section 7(1) of the Criminal Justice (Money Laundering and Financing Terrorism) Act 2010***

Criminal Sanctions for money laundering are up to 14 YEARS and/or a fine on indictment or 1 year summary and/or a fine of up to €5,000.

All financial Institutions must report transactions over €15,000

Other types of white collar crime

Other forms of white collar crimes include:

1. Insurance fraud by insurance sellers and claimants
2. Credit card fraud
3. Customs fraud
4. Pension scheme fraud
5. Time share and retirement home fraud.

White collar crimes are normally committed by less powerful businessmen and fraudsters, these types of financial frauds don't normally affect the economy negatively, and also a higher rate of prosecutions.

Theories of Violent Crime

Fear of crime has been defined by Ferraro: (1995) as

> *"an emotional response of dread or anxiety to crime or symbols that a person associates with crime."*

Fear of crime is not just the fear of violent to the person, it extend to the property, family and friends etc, it makes people feel vulnerable and in turn can cause an impact on a person's quality of life.

Murder

Murder is one of the greatest fears of most members of society; however it must be noted that although a heinous crime and socially unacceptable it is now an almost daily occurrence when as early as the 1980s to hear of a murder in Ireland drew breath of horror, nowadays it at best gets a "that's awful" or "what is the world coming to".

Murder is the most serious offence which can be perpetrated, it is an act which if found guilty will find the offender getting a minimum sentence of life.

Murder can be defined as premediated, or intentional with malice aforethought,(intention to kill and prepare for it) and manslaughter which is intentional or accidentally without malice aforethought,(no intention, no preparations), manslaughter can be voluntary (illegal, not self-defence etc) or involuntary (kill another person while committing another crime such as burglary of robbery)

Gang Crime

Ireland and the UK shared on criminal family for decades, the Dundon Gang from Limerick Ireland had spent over 30 years living in London, here the families reputation as gang leaders was cemented in 2003 when Kenneth snr was officially placed on Scotland Yard's most wanted, their MO was burglary and intimidation. All bar two of Kenneth's children followed in his footsteps into crime and John Dundon came to Ireland in 2007 and continued the family tradition of gangland violence, John was arrested and sentenced for the murder of Shane Geoghegan who was mistaken for John McNamara, his arch rival in 2008. Four out of the six Dundon children are incarcerated in Ireland for gangland violence.

The history of gangs

Gangs in the 50s and 60's in the UK and the USA was in the form of the Kray twins in the UK and the Mafia in the USA. These gangs were all about the money, this money came from protection rackets, prostitution and smuggling, and these feuds were also about control.

Modern gangs

Modern gangs are more about "turf" about control of particular areas, it is about honour and respect, hits on rival gangs are often ordered due to one member feeling disrespected or dishonoured. It is also found that many young people enter gangs with the intent of finding where they belong, looking for the security and sense of belonging or an alternative to "family".

Theories of criminal behaviour.

Can we discuss crime without asking the age old question: ***what causes it to occur?***

Criminal and forensic psychology is the study of why individuals commit crimes, the theories of what made them do the crime (psychologically) (Mens Rea, guilty mind) and why they behave (act) in certain ways (Actus Reus, guilty act). By understanding why a person commits a crime, ways can be developed to control crime or rehabilitate the offender. There are many theories in criminology. Some theorists say that crime is relative to the individual; they believe that an individual weights the pros and cons and makes a conscious choice whether or not to commit a crime. Others believe it is the community's responsibility to ensure that the residents do not commit crime by offering them a safe and secure place in which to live. Some theorists believe that some individuals have hereditary traits that will determine how they will react when put in certain hostile conditions. By studying these theories and applying them to individuals, it is hoped that psychologists can deter criminals from being recidivistic and help in their rehabilitation.

In Order to understand criminal behaviour we need to understand what factors are connected with or "cause" the criminals to do the crime. Gardai, the Judiciary, the prison service and probationary services strive to understand the theories of crime and provide information. Knowing something about the factors associated with criminal behaviour, the characteristics of offender types, and the "causes" of crime provides information with which to:

- Pursue and investigate suspects
- Adjudicate defendants, determine the level of sentencing

- Manage offenders in correctional institutions, make parole and re-entry decisions, and to design crime prevention and crime control strategies.

Neuropsychology and Crime

Some of the most contested theories within forensic psychology which aim to identify the factors in determining why people crime, start with neuropsychology.

Approximately 46%-50% of forensic psychologists said that they used neuropsychological assessment mechanisms in their pre-trial evaluations.[28](Borum R, Grisso T. 1995)

Neuropsychology is literally defined as the study of brain to behaviour relationship.[29] (Sesta. J)

---

[28] Borum R, Grisso T. 1995;Psychological test use in criminal forensic evaluations. 26:465-473

[29] Joseph J. Sesta, 2010; Ph.D., M.S.Pharm., American Board of Professional Neuropsychology. Suite 206
Riverview, Florida 33569

Psychoanalytic theorists and the origins of crime

Psychoanalysis

Henry Maudsley (1835–1918): Maudsley concluded that criminals were suffering from "moral degeneracy," a deficiency of moral sense.

Sigmund Freud (1856–1939): Human behaviour can be explained by examining early childhood experiences. Sigmund Freud is the father of neuropsychological analysis and his theories formed the basis for future theorists, some to prove his finding and those who disproved many of his theories. Freud only ever worked with adults looking back on childhood experiences, he never worked with children. Therefore there could be problems with accuracy due to the human's inability to reproduce accurate memories or "eye witness testimony" (Munsterburg). Freud's insistence on sticking to the theories of the criminal behaviour stem from the childhood were quickly ruled out and caused a weakness in his theories. However, his three parts to the human "being" or "the personality" are still being used.

Freud's theories suggest that we are driven by the EGO, the SUPER EGO and the ID.

The ID is the unconscious thought, the instant gratification, for instance, sex or violence, it's the theory of "if it feels good then do it". (Lester & Van Voorhis, cited in, Criminology: Theory, Research, and Policy; Gennaro Vito, Jeffrey Maahs)[30]

---

30 Vito. G, Maahs. J, 2011; Criminology: Theory, Research, and Policy. Jones & Bartlett

Superego, this can be describes as your conscious, from moral reasoning, “lying is wrong” to self-reasoning or self-awareness “when I grow up I want to be just like mummy”.

Ego: known as the “psychological thermostat” that regulates the wishes of the personal wishes of the id with the social restrictions of the superego.

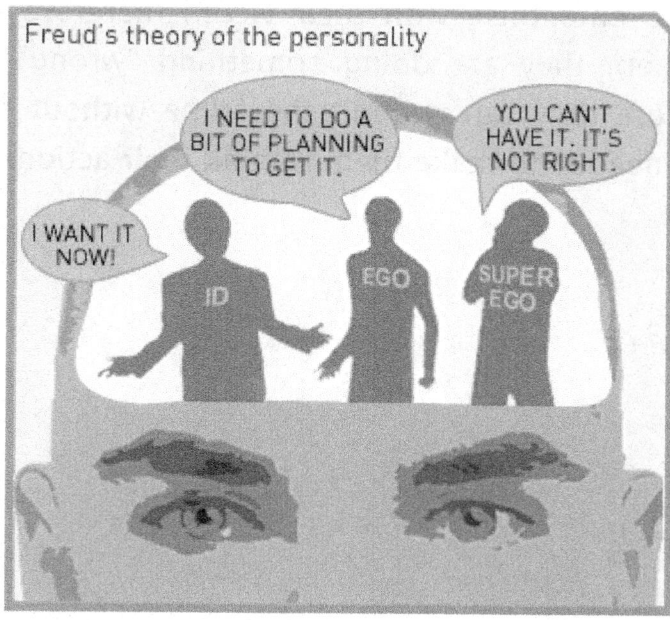

[31]

Freud’s theories also claimed that Human nature is inherently antisocial, insofar as; Id: infants start life with antisocial drives; Superego: forms from experience; Ego: helps to negotiate demands for instant gratification with acceptable behaviour.

---

[31] http://revisewithrachie.com/revision-sheets/abnormality/the-psychodynamic-model-of-abnormality/

If the ego is not strong enough to stabilise the demands of the **ID** and the **SUPEREGO** then behavioural deviation will follow.

I.E. if a person's **ID** is stronger than their **EGO** then this could give them a tendency to becoming a rapist in later life due to their having a stronger pleasure drive than SUPEREGO.

Take for instance a psychopath, they are unable to process guilt and they have no ability to empathise with their victim therefore the **SUPEREGO** who is telling them they are doing something "wrong" simply is not processed therefore they can commit the crime without the feelings of empathy or guilt needed to make them rethink their actions.

Sexual Offenders

Sexual offenders are typically seen as a similar group of offenders. However, it is well established nowadays that there is unlimited variety amongst sex offenders (Bartol & Bartol, 2011).

- type of sexual activity,
- age,
- background,
- attitudes,
- beliefs,
- personality,
- religion.

Also there are differences in the types of victims, the use of violence and the degree of planning. They rarely stop at sexual crimes and have been known to have an array of crimes they are charged with when arrested.

Adolescent males perpetrate 20–30% of all rapes, and 30–50% of all child molestations (Becker & Johnson, 2001). 70% of adolescent sex offenders come from two-parent homes, attend school and are successful, and don't suffer from any kind of mental disorder (Becker & Johnson, 2001). It is becoming more apparent that preadolescents (boys and girls) also commit sexual offences.

Sexual aggression can be observed in children as young as 3 or 4. A very large proportion of preadolescent girls carry out acts of sexual violence. Their behaviour is just as aggressive as that seen in boys. The victims of preadolescent offenders are typically very young (4–7) and the victim is known to the offender (sibling, friend, acquaintance). Very little is known about why such young children sexually offend.

Rape

Acquaintance Rape ("date rape") is very common - as high as 60% of all rape cases. The UN has reported that sexual abuse of women and girls is rampant across many parts of the undeveloped world - e.g. Afghanistan, Saudi Arabia, Somalia, Chile, India. In the western world, the U.S. has the highest incidence of rape. The FBI reported 71,857 rapes in 2004 - 5% of all violent crime. 9% of reported rapes were committed against males and 1% are female-to-female rapes. The true figure however is vastly higher as most rapes go unreported which makes it extremely difficult to obtain accurate figures. Just think about the abuse within the Catholic Church in Ireland and across the world and the incidence of prison rapes as well as the incidence of marital rape.[32]

Data about perpetrators of rape crimes comes from convicted felons which need to be considered in light of the fact that only 3% of reported rapes result in conviction. These individuals are therefore a very unrepresentative sample. Rapists tend to be young with 43% under 25 and 15% under 15. 5% were under 15 (11% for all sexual offences). This appears to be a massive underestimation however as other findings suggest at least 30% of rapes are committed by early adolescents (Cellini, 1995).

A consistent finding is that rapists have continual and repeated violations of the law. Scully and Marola (1984) found that 82% of rapists had a prior criminal record. Only 23% had previously been convicted of a sexual offence.

Many rapists are unemployed and two-thirds are unmarried which is in contrast to paedophiles where two-thirds are married and most are employed. Large scale research studies (e.g. Black & Pettway, 2001) found

[32] https://en.wikipedia.org/wiki/Rape_statistics

that very few rapists reoffend sexually following release from prison. 1.3% of rapists were rearrested for another sex crime within 6 months of release (Langan et al., 2003). After three years, 5% of rapists were rearrested for another sex crime. However, 41% were rearrested for a nonsexual crime after 3 years and 15% of these were for violent crimes not including rape or sexual offences. Rapists have been classified in terms of their perceptions of their crimes: Deniers and Admitters.

Admitters are those who accept full responsibility for their actions and fully corroborate the account of their victim. Deniers justify their rape behaviour by making the victim blameworthy and ultimately responsible. Their account of the rape incident typically differs considerably from that of the victim[33].

Five themes run through deniers justifications.[34]

1. Women are seductresses,
2. Women really mean yes when they say no,
3. Most women relax and actually enjoy it,
4. Nice girls don't get raped,
5. Rape is a minor offence since the person is not physically hurt.[35]

Most deniers characterise the victim as the aggressor; as ultimately responsible because they didn't protest enough; and that she deep down wanted it to happen and greatly enjoyed it.

---

[33] MASCULINITIES, SEXUALITIES AND CHILD SEXUAL ABUSE BY ANNE ISABEL COSSINS http://www.austlii.edu.au/au/journals/UNSWLawTD/1998/4.pdf

[34] Anne Cossins - MASCULINITIES, SEXUALITIES AND CHILD SEXUAL ABUSE http://www.austlii.edu.au/au/journals/UNSWLawTD/1998/4.pdf

[35] CONVICTED RAPIST'S VOCABULARY OF MOTIVE EXCUSES AND JUSTIFICATIONS - Diana Scully and Joseph Marolla - https://www.d.umn.edu/~bmork/2306/readings/scullyandmarollis.htm

Biological Theories of crime

Adoption Studies. Studies that have been done with children reared by biological parents compared to their siblings or twins reared by adoptive parents in an attempt to demonstrate a genetic link to criminal behaviour. Results have been mixed.

Genetic – Twin Studies

- An 'MZ apart' study is when two monozygotic children have been brought up apart. If both turn out to be criminals then this would be support for the genetic explanation. The degree of similarity between two twins is known as the concordance rate. This rate can then be compared with dizygotic twins ('DZ together') who are brought up together
- Looking at a number of studies the average concordance rate is 55% for MZ twins and 17% for DZ twins (Bartol, 1999).

Genetic – Adoption Studies

- If a child who has criminal parents is adopted and later the child becomes a criminal then this will lend support to the genetic explanation.
- A study by Schulsinger (1972) found that only 3.9% of such children developed criminal tendencies. This was compared with control children (adopted children from non-criminal biological parents), where 1.4% became criminal. The small difference was not significant. The sample was large at 57, so there was a good prospect of detecting significance. The psychopathy was loosely defined as impulse-ridden behaviour.
- Crowe (1974) found that in a sample of 52 adopted children of imprisoned women; seven of them had at least one criminal

conviction, by comparison with only one in a matched control group.

- Mednick et al (1987) found 14,000 adoptees amongst court convictions. Many had criminal biological parents (particularly strong relationship for sons and fathers). There was no relationship in the types of crime committed. Improved social conditions reduced crime (going against the genetic explanation).

Autonomic Nervous System (ANS). Mednick's theory that individuals who inherit a slower than normal autonomic nervous system learn to control aggressive or antisocial behaviour slowly or not at all. This leads to increased violence and criminal activity.

Criminaloid. One of three criminal types identified by Lombroso. The criminaloid is motivated by passion, and will commit criminal acts under the proper circumstances.

Determinism. In considering biological theories, determinism refers to the view that an individual's criminal lifestyle or actions is the direct result of genetic inheritance or biological predisposition. Soft determinism, as explained by Matza, examines the role of determinism, but also acknowledges that other factors, from environmental to choice, may be part of the equation.

This assumes that behaviour is not completely and strictly determined by the individual's genetic or biological makeup.

Evolutionary Theory. A broad-based view that certain types of criminal behaviour are genetic and passed down from one generation to the next through evolutionary processes of natural selection and survival.

Gene-Based Evolutionary Theory. A general approach that suggests that the process of natural selection has resulted in criminal genetic tendencies that are passed down from generation to generation.

Insane Criminal. One of three criminal types identified by Lombroso. The insane criminal type includes idiots, imbeciles, epileptics, psychotics, and the mentally unstable. These criminals are unable to control their actions; however, they do not possess the stigmata or identifying characteristics of the born criminal.

Stigmata. Characteristics claimed by Lombroso that could be used to identify the "born criminal." They include things such as extra fingers or toes, large lips, receding chins, excessive skin wrinkles, and large monkey-like ears.

Intelligence and Learning in Criminology

Intelligence: capacity to act purposefully, think rationally and deal effectively with the environment

- Culture-bound concept: skills necessary for success in a culture
- Lombroso hypothesized that his criminals were "feebleminded", but there were no measure of intelligence
- Binet: first intelligence test
- Used the concept of mental age: if the majority of children of a given age can complete a task, the task requires that mental age.
- Problem: MA does not change after mid-adolescence but chronological age does. Thus, using Binet's test, everyone would become feebleminded

Goddard's work was discredited

- It was until the 1970s that the issue of intelligence and crime was reconsidered by criminologists
- He tested children, compared mental age to chronological age
- 10-15 point gap between offenders and non-offenders: 100 v. 87
- More than 10% of prisoners are MR, while the percentage in the general population is less than 3%
- Is this because of social class differences between prisoners and the general population?

Studies of non-delinquent and delinquent adolescents matched for age, social class and ethnic groups also find an IQ difference, although not as large,

- Lower IQ scores are associated with higher recidivism among offenders

- Most of the differences are for Verbal IQ rather than Performance IQ
- Higher IQ, especially verbal, might mean that one understands consequences better and have better planning skills--protective factor
- A lower verbal IQ might mean that the person is less likely to use "internal speech" and be more impulsive (and thus less likely to be deterred)
- The brighter might get arrested less often (although self-report studies still support a difference)
- Higher verbal IQ is associated with better moral reasoning skills

School problems hypothesis:

- Low verbal IQ -- poor academic achievement -- frustration -- truancy and dropping out -- association with other dropouts, unemployment - crime

- Learning a relatively permanent change, due to experience, that can affect behaviour

Human behaviour is learned, and learned by:

- classical conditioning

- operant conditioning

Crime addictions

(Peale. S, 1985) "addictive experiences are potent modifiers of mood and sensation". [36]

There is a common theory that the following characteristics of addictions include:[37]

- Tolerance - the need for more to produce the same effect.
- Withdrawal - distress after a period of non-engagement.
- Craving - distress associated with desire to re-engage.
- Salience - increasing importance of addiction in lifestyle.
- Conflict - increasing awareness of negative consequences.
- Relapse - reinstatement after a decision to stop or reduce.

(Peale. S, 1985) "***addictive experiences are potent modifiers of mood and sensation".***

There is a common theory that the following characteristics of addictions include:

- Tolerance - the need for more to produce the same effect.
- Withdrawal - distress after a period of non-engagement.
- Craving - distress associated with desire to re-engage.
- Salience - increasing importance of addiction in lifestyle.
- Conflict - increasing awareness of negative consequences.
- Relapse - reinstatement after a decision to stop or reduce.

---

[36] PEELE, S.(1985) The Meaning of Addiction: Compulsive Experience and its Interpretation.
Lexington MA, Lexington Books.
[37] Hodge. J; http://www.offenders-anonymous.org.uk/section.html?secpath=01.08.&pgid=1

Tolerance

As with any behaviour whether negative or positive the tolerance levels are key. A runner who runs one mile today may feel that one mile tomorrow is insufficient, they may need to run 1.1 miles to get the same emotional feelings from the run. This is the same with criminality, Criminals may become more and more tolerant to their own behaviour and the acts may need to increase in order to obtain the same desired effect.

Withdrawal

As with any addiction crime also has withdrawal symptoms. When a smoker stops smoking they may feel agitated, irritated and even upset to a point of anger or fear. They may feel that the feelings are so intense that the only way to relieve them is to smoke a cigarette. This is true for other addictions, such as crime, undertaking another "job" may relieve those withdrawal symptoms.

Craving

When the body has a craving, there is a longing, a longing to commit the crime, smoke the cigarette, run the extra mile. When the craving becomes stronger the withdrawal symptoms in turn increase the craving for the activity, For instance, I want, I want I want.

Salience

Salience, when not committing the crimes the offender may be daydreaming about it, planning it or even executing it in their minds

Euphoria / relief / mood regulation

The feel good feeling an addicts gets when they "give in" to their cravings and partake in the behaviour i.e. smoking, drinking, running, crime. They get a "feel good" response from the actions.

Conflict

When a person undertakes behaviour they "know" they should not be undertaking they often feel inner conflict, they know what they are doing is wrong, and yet they continue with that behaviour.

Relapse

As with any addiction the person may feel that they will "give up or stop" the addiction or behaviour, they may feel that it is not legally, morally or personally right to be partaking in the behaviour so they take the decision to stop. However, like some addictions crime is incredible difficult to stop and offenders regularly reoffend or relapse after deciding not to do it again.

Recognising criminal addictions

How is it possible to recognise addicted offenders? The characteristics are a starting point, the factors defined above, if a burglar commits more and more elaborate break-ins, and in essence the appearance of a motivational factor is evident from the details it could be discussed how the offender is addicted to committing the act rather than any other reason, in essence it could be said that if addicted to crime offenders are identified then the rehabilitation could be more successful. It may also be evident in incarceration facilities when offenders are reluctant to be released, as they know that they will reoffend and have a personal knowledge of their addiction therefore creating conflict, and they may have made a concerted decision not to reoffend while when released they relapse because the craving is too overwhelming.

For some types of offence, for example joyriding or shoplifting, its role may be minimal since the offence behaviour itself is capable of frequent expression, while for other types of offence, such as certain sexual offences, fantasy may be the central component driving the offending through the mechanism of tolerance.

A Theoretical Model of Behaviour Addictions for Addictive Offenders adapted by Brown (1997)

Specialisation in a single offence or a narrow range of similar offences. It is unlikely that anyone can be addicted to crime as a whole or to a range of criminal activities which might be expected to provide widely differencing subjective emotional experiences.

Individual vulnerabilities of the person involved similar to those identified for addictions - for example, poor relationships and a restricted range of easily-accessible rewarding activities.

Powerful emotional reaction experienced by the individual in association with the criminal act which is mood-changing - colloquially, a strong 'buzz' for the individual. Increasing salience of the criminal activity so that, even when it is not being committed, it is being planned or fantasised about and all of life, thinking, feeling and behaviour is dominated by and organised around the next opportunity to offend.

Positive feedback loops promoting increasing and repeated offending, like conflict narrowing the range of easily-accessible alternative rewarding activities, tolerance escalating the risks to be taken to achieve the same escape, withdrawals leading to restlessness and irritability when offending is not possible, and relief offending arising out of the need to block despair and guilt from the last offence by beginning preoccupation with the next.

- Cycles of criminal activity – corresponding to cycles of need to use the criminal activity to manage hedonic tone in the offender.
- Low self-esteem – subjective feelings of loss of control, unable to cut down offending or be abstinent.
- Rituals before or after offending – a series of routines or chains of stimuli, responses, actions which seem to build up or break down arousal.
- Disconnection from normal flow of mental life – offence feels it is being committed in a 'time capsule' apart from ordinary life.
- Patterns of reoffending which look like relapse in the addictions – ie, involves fantasies stimulated by relapse-provoking situations which become progressively more extreme and dominant as the offence is approached.
- Occasional reinstatement phenomena – even after many years of remission, a rapid reversion to the frequency and intensity of offending which was characteristic of offending at its height, perhaps many years before.

Media and Crime

Is Crime distorted in the media? What is the sources of the stories which claim to be research based or what truth is there behind the masses of criminal stories and statistics which we reading our papers and online news sources and feeds every day?

The Media Representation of Crime

The media does not care about statistics and qualitative or quantitative research, it is concerned with selling papers, magazines, tv and moves, therefore the portrayal of crime and statistical analysis of crimes should be "taken with a pinch of salt" when discussing crimes and criminal statistics.

Are newspapers and magazines feed societies fear of crime and in essence creating a catch 22 or loop situation? Skogan (1987) stated that

> *"a high level of fear of crime often appears not only in those who are more likely to be victimised, such as the poor and those living in inner city areas, but also those who enjoy comparatively low levels of recorded victimisation, such as women and the elderly".*

The statistics give an insight into the portrayal of crime, and shockingly over 75% of those who were asked about what they had just read or seen in the news believed that the media's interpretation of the crimes was accurate. Graber (1980)

The effects of this media portrayal of crime has a worrying reaction from many members of society, such as removing and withdrawing from society, not going out as much, taking excessive precautions in safety in areas know to suffer with excessive criminal activity, explain that

> *"for those fearing victimisation, each excursion beyond the relative safety of home is like walking through a minefield - at any moment, a purse may be snatched, a body assaulted, a sense of dignity affronted".* Box et al. (1988)

Generally, the media are seen as exaggerating the risks associated with crime and criminal behaviours and this is believed to be done in an effort to increase sentences and make punishments harsher.

Statistics for media coverage

- Crimes of violence are disproportionately covered:
- Murder: accounts for 1/3rd of all reports.[38]
- Burglary received less coverage than murder
- 64.5% of newspaper crime stories are violent[39] despite 6% of all convicted crimes being violent
- Fatal crime accounted for 38-53% of crime stories.[40]

From the above statistics it can be seen that fatality, killing, horrific deaths and murder sell stories, as does the medias need to ensure we are aware of the offenders "social status, i.e. poor, unemployed, ethnicity and male etc."

The media tend to focus on sensationalist, prurient, and moralistic stories reflects the desires of the general public[41] therefore the old adage sites true, *"believe half of what you see, and none of what you hear"*

---

[38] (Reiner 2000)

[39] Williams and Dickinson (1989)

[40] Cumberbatch (1995)

[41] Laissez-Faire Theories

The media can heighten fear and perceptions amongst the general public, it can also be seen to enforce notions of the theories of crime, by using the following;

Labelling Theory:

- The media establishes stereotypes and social beliefs of criminality, through labelling those are criminals, or criminal types the media establishes and reinforce labels.

Deviancy Theory

- The media identifies the types of deviant groups which are then reinforced by alienation. Fear of those deviants are then portrayed and amplified.[42]

Strain Theory

- The media, and in particular advertising, is central to the establishment of people's goals: economic goals.[43]

---

[42] Jackson, J., and Gray, E. (2010). 'Functional fear and public insecurities about crime'. British Journal of Criminology 50(1): 1-22

[43] Kahn-Harris, K. (eds.) After subculture: Critical studies in contemporary youth culture. Basingstoke: Palgrave Macmillan

Chapter four

The Irish Legal System

Article 38 of the Irish Constitution guarantees every citizen the right to a fair trial.

What is "Law"?

It is possible to describe law as the body of official rules and regulations, generally found in constitutions, legislation, judicial opinions, etc., they are used to govern a society and to control the behaviour of members within society, so therefore, and law is a recognised instrument of social control.

Explanation; *Every country needs a legal system so that people can live in peace and free from worry about being attacked or imprisoned, stolen from or harmed emotionally or physically. A legal system is a guide for a group of people, cultures, and societies to live within a municipal system. The law governs how society behaves towards each other. The aim and objective of laws and regulations is to include protecting the rights of all citizens.*

Brehon Law

Irish History has had a great effect on the laws of the land. Ireland has a history of bloody invasions and tyrannical reign over its people, from the Viking invaders, to the Norman invasions to the British conquests, none more so than the British invasion of the 17th Century when the old Brehon (the old name in for lawgiver) legal system was abolished by Queen Elizabeth the 1st, claiming it was barbaric and unreasonable and even barbarous. The Brehon system was overseen by representatives, these were taken from the community, they were; the chief, poet, historian, landowner, bishop, professor of literature, professor of law, a noble, and a lay vicar, it was these representatives that made and changed the laws, these laws covered every conceivable aspect of daily life in Ireland, it referred to the behaviours within each community and each community could have different laws. The richer the person the more legal standing they would have within the community, this was also held to be classless, as the Kings and High Kings would have to adhere to the laws of the Brehons the same as any menial labourer. Richer members of society were held more accountable for their actions than a poorer, if a rich farmer stole a cow from a poor farmer, his fine would be a lot more severe than if the poor farmer had stolen from the rich. In Brehon times in Ireland women were equal to men, they were Queens, led their armies into battles, they were poets, doctors and were able to bring cases against other people, it was the reign of Queen Elizabeth 1st ironically that led to the ending of Brehon laws and with them the rights of women.

An example of some of the strange and abstract Brehon laws which were in existence, (taking into account most of these laws were written down by St Patrick and when people still lived in mud huts and life revolved around the commune)

Examples of Brehon Laws; how people interacted with each other.

- February first is the day on which husband and wife may decide to walk away from the marriage.
- When you become old the family must provide you with one oatcake a day plus a container of sour milk. They must bathe you every 20th night and wash the head every Saturday. Seventeen sticks of firewood is the allotment for keeping you warm.

- No fools, drunks or female scolds are allowed in the doctor's house when a patient is healing there. No bad news to be brought and no talking across the bed. No grunts of pigs or barking of dogs outside.
- A husband who through listlessness does not go to his wife in her bed must pay a fine.
- If a pregnant woman craves a morsel of food and her husband withholds it though stinginess or neglect he must pay a fine.
- Whoever comes to the door you must feed him and care for him with no questions asked.

Explanation; *the Brehons, or 'brithemuin', were like the judges or jurists of today, however we can describe Brehons as being similar to mediators. Their role was to ensure a stable society by a series and system of fines, there was no prison time, nor corporal (physical) punishment, if you behaved against the rules you paid a fine, it was as simple as that. A person could go to the home and demand that you pay then what you owe them and you could not leave the home until it was paid, if you injured someone you had to pay their way until they healed, food etc. This was originally thought to be a system of barbaric rules, however on investigation in modern times Brehon law is deemed to be one of the most sophisticated of its time anywhere in Europe which was based on the theory of natural law (fair, just and reasonable) whereby people were put before property no matter what the class or how much wealth you had.*

The Four sources of Irish law

1. The Constitution
2. European Community law
3. Common law
4. Legislation

Source one – The Irish Constitution

The primary source of law in Ireland until Ireland joined the EU was the Irish Constitution.

The Irish Constitution was enacted by a popular plebiscite (*a vote of the common people*) held on 1 July 1937, and came into force on 29 December 1937. (*The Constitution is a written document which governs how Ireland should be run; it documents the rights, privileges and responsibilities of the Irish citizens and State).*

The Irish Constitution can only be amended by referendum (*vote*) of the people (*by plebiscite*). A proposal to amend the Constitution is introduced into Dáil Éireann as a bill and if passed by the Dáil, once this bill is passed it is then put to the people.

Article 15.2.1 of the Irish Constitution states: *The sole power of making law is given to Oireachtas (everyone in the Dáil, Fianna Fail Fine Gael, Labour etc). Explicitly states that "**no other** legislative authority has power to make laws for the State."*[44]

When the people agree to the changes to the Constitution the President signs the referendum bill into law.

Article 25 of the Irish Constitution states that: *"The President must sign a Bill into law."* And

Article 25.2.1 of the Irish Constitution states: *"that the President to sign such a Bill into law not earlier than the fifth and not later than the seventh day after the date in which it is presented to him".*

There laws introduced by the Constitution are called Articles, some of the major rights afforded by the Constitution are, the right to life, the right to

---

[44] http://www.irishstatutebook.ie/en/constitution/

assembly, the right to fair procedures, the right to a family life, to name a few. ***Article 50 of the Constitution of Ireland*** allowed all laws that had been in force in the Irish Free State prior to its coming into force on 29 December 1937. The president can refer any bill to the Supreme Court under Article 26 of the constitution for clarification of any terms which may be ambiguous (*unclear*) before signing the bill into legislation or statute law. The president then signs the Bill into law, however, the President can refuse to sign a Bill into law under

Article 26 of the Irish Constitution if they deem the Bill unconstitutional or under **Article 27 of the Irish Constitution** if the Seanad have refused to pass the Bill if the Dáil have invoked **Article 23 of the Irish Constitution** (passing a Bill even if the Seanad refuse to)[45]

[45] IBID

Source two - European Community Law

Ireland has a Common Law Legal System with a written constitution, this constitution provides that the Oireachtas may use statutory instruments in order to implement European Union law, this power derived from the *European Communities Act, 1972,* (as amended) which stated that statutory instruments have effect as if they were primary legislation.[46]

Ireland's membership of the European Community requires that Ireland accommodates EC legislation in its entirety, therefore, Ireland agrees to the Supremacy of EC law. Ireland must implement EC legislation taking account of Irelands Constitution. The European Union is supported by five principle institutions.

1. The European Commission;
2. The Council of European Union;
3. The European Parliament;
4. The European Court of Justice;
5. The European Court of Auditors

[46] *European Communities Act, 1972*
http://www.irishstatutebook.ie/eli/1972/act/27/enacted/en/html

The laws of the EC derive from treaties.

The European Community Treaties

1957 - The Treaty of Rome (the founding treaty)

1987 - The Single European Act (to remove trade barriers)

1993 - The Maastricht Treaty (creation of EU citizenship and EU Currency)

1997 - The Amsterdam Treaty (creation of jobs within the EU, this Treaty set out plans to be implemented by each member to tackle unemployment throughout the EU)

2001- The Nice Treaty (set out the division of power within the EU for each member country)

2009 - The Lisbon Treaty (recognised each countries responsibilities to the Human Rights Act and made it legally binding on member Countries, it made responsibility **more** transparent i.e. accountability for each countries actions and the impact it has on the EU). These treaties are the primary source of EC law, however on a day to day basic Regulations and Directives are the pieces of legislation which are called Secondary legislation.

Article 249 of the EC Treaty

Article 249 of the EC Treaty states that the *"European Parliament acting jointly with the Council, the Council and the Commission shall make* *regulations and issue directives, take decisions, make recommendations or deliver opinions"*[47]

Laws approved by the institutions of the EC through the procedures defined within the Treaties are known as secondary legislation. ***Article 249*** states that it is the responsibility of the EC Institutions to enact secondary legislation, these secondary legislations are:

[47] Treaty establishing the European Community (Nice consolidated version) Part Five: Institutions of the Community Title I: Provisions governing the institutions http://eur-lex.europa.eu/LexUriServ/LexUriServ.do?uri=CELEX:12002E249:EN:HTML

Regulations

A regulation shall have general application. It shall be binding in its entirety and directly applicable in all Member States. EU Regulations are directly binding in all Member States (binding from Europe, not Ireland, there is no need for Ireland to introduce new legislation to give effect to the new regulation as it is binding from Europe and does not need local implementation). Member States are required to introduce procedures for their implementation, such as penalties or fines. It is binding in its entirety, no member Country can decide if there are bits or pieces of the Regulation they wish to enact, they have to abide by it in its entirety (completely)

Directives.

A directive shall be binding, as to the result to be achieved, upon each Member State to which it is addressed, but shall leave to the national authorities the choice of form and methods. Directives are binding *"as the result to be achieved, upon each Member State to which it is addressed, but shall leave to the national authorities the choice of form and methods."*

*(**Example:** EC Directives are binding on all Member States as to the **objectives to be achieved within a certain time limit**. But they are not binding in their entirety; this means it is up to each Country to enact legislation to give effect to the directives intentions keeping their own Countries requirements, i.e. a regulation for a set minimum wage in every EC Country would not be viable. For instance, if a set minimum wage was introduced into Europe as €4.50 per hour, and this was directly binding on all member states then this could cause a lot of hardship in some Countries. i.e. €4.50 per hour may be a wage that is sufficient in one Country but defiantly not in Ireland where the cost of living is so much higher, this is why the set minimum wage in Europe is a Directive, each*

*Country has the ability to set its own minimum wage according to the cost of living. In Ireland it is presently €8.65 per hour, nonetheless it **MUST** have a minimum wage, that's the purpose of the directive).*

Decisions.

Decisions are binding in their entirety (Completely) on those persons/bodies/Countries that the Decisions are addressed, be it a Member State, a Country, an organisation or an individual. They do not need to be implemented into National Law.

Recommendations.

Recommendations have no binding force. Recommendations are not binding but express the Councils or Commissions view on policy to the Member States or to the individuals to which they are addressed. Whilst not legally binding, they have political and moral significance and can be preliminary requirements to subsequent mandatory rules.

Opinions.

Opinions have no binding force. Opinions are not binding but express the Councils or Commissions view on policy to the Member States or to the individuals to which they are addressed. Whilst not legally binding, they have political and moral significance and can be preliminary requirements to subsequent mandatory rules.

Source three - Common Law

After the abolishment of the Irish Brehon laws Ireland became governed by what was then the British system of Common Law. The then Queen Elizabeth I, wanted a uniform legal system, Common law was not just used by the British ruling sovereignty, this law originated with the Normans. Common law is the process whereby a body of laws arises from precedent (what went before, let it stand) the decisions in previous cases are binding on future cases of the same standing (materially similar in nature). Precedent *"the doctrine of binding precedent"* is also known as *"State Decisis"* (*stand by the decision*) there are many translations for stare decisis but in plain English it means, a decision of a higher court binds all lower courts.

The decision in court is divided into two distinct parts, firstly the *"ratio decidendi"* (*the reason for the decision, the reason for the guilty or not guilty verdict*) and *"obiter dictum"* (*something said by the way, something the judge may have said*), such as, in a recent Monaghan District Court hearing the Judge said that he would not be granting orders against debtors, "*because the banks **were not negotiating** with debtors to come to an agreement"* (*Ratio Decidendi*), and the banks can "*go whistle for their money"* (*obiter dictum*)). It must be noted that the obiter dictum is not binding; it is the ratio decidendi that creates the precedent which binds lower courts. Civil cases are brought by individuals against individuals and Criminal cases are brought by the DPP (Director of Public Prosecutions) on behalf of the State. However, the obiter may be persuasive (*taken into consideration*)

In Ireland there are some exceptions to the right of private individuals to bring a criminal case against another individual

(**Example:** *Any person who has a clear and unambiguous complaint against another citizen can make an application to a District Court Judge* *and put forward their evidence and request permission to issue a criminal summons*).[48]

The standard of proof (*how much proof is needed to be successful*) for the issue of a criminal summons is lower than that in a DPP case and those who were summonsed would, in all essence, have to make a challenge to the proof. But, most criminal prosecutions originate by the Director of Public Prosecutions on behalf of the State. The Director is a State official but is independent of Government in the performance of his or her functions.

The system of Common law in Ireland is by and for a successful one, there are those who advocate that it is staunch and unfair, others who say it is very far too strict and judges are not allowed to use their discretion when cases are significantly similar yet the circumstances are different. Others believe that helps those to have some idea of how their case will go, what the outcome may be, therefore making for a plan of action as to the outcome of their own case.

***(Explanation:** Common law was the decisions of Judges which was written down and the decisions then recorded in the court journals. These judgements were then used so that all law in the law was "Common" or the same everywhere in the Country; this ensured that the law was consistent. Common law precedent, (previous decisions of higher courts which were binding on all lower courts) may have been overturned by a higher court, i.e. the High Court may overturn a decision of the Circuit Court. Therefore it is important that the legal representative knows the status of any precedent which may affect their client, this is why there is searches done in court journals.)*

---

48 Information Ireland. (2012, October). The Irish State - Legal System. Retrieved from http://www.ireland-information.com/reference/legalsys.html.

Source four – Acts of the Oireachtas or Legislation

There are two types of Legislation

1. Primary legislation
2. Secondary legislation

Primary Legislation

Article 15.2.1 of the Irish Constitution states: *The sole power of making law is given to Oireachtas. Explicitly states that* ***"no other"*** *legislative authority has power to make laws for the State."* [49]

The sole and exclusive power (*no other bodies or states can make laws for Ireland*) of making laws for the State is vested in the Oireachtas (*Parliament*) subject to the obligations of European Union Membership as provided in the Constitution of Ireland. The Oireachtas consists of the President and two Houses, Dáil Éireann (House of Representatives) and Seanad Éireann (Senate).

All Legislation in Ireland has beginnings as a bill (a draft of the proposed law), this bill starts as either a private members bill (rare in Ireland, these bills are introduced into the Oireachtas or Seanad by a member of the government, "these rarely pass") and public members bills.(the most common type, these are bills that would affect the populous, or the greatest amount of members of the pubic and introduced by government bodies).

Bills can be introduced in either the Dáil or Seanad. (Normally the Dáil) There are five stages to a bill becoming legislation.

---

[49]http://www.irishstatutebook.ie/en/constitution/

Once a Bill has been passed by both Houses, although it is not necessary for the Seanad to agree by virtue of **Article 23 of the Irish Constitution**[50] which states that the Dáil has the power to pass a resolution deeming the Bill passed even if the Seanad reject it, or in the event that the Seanad do not decide on the fate of a Bill within 90 days the Dáil has the power again to deem it passed by resolution. Once this occurs the Taoiseach presents a vellum copy (calf skin) of the Bill prepared in the Office of the Houses of the Oireachtas to the President for signature and declaration as a law.

Delegated/secondary legislation

When an bill becomes law it becomes and Act, this act then confers powers on the relevant minister to make changes or amendments to the act, this means that parts inside the act can be changed without the act itself being changed, thus saving Government time, notwithstanding the financial savings of not have a whole piece of legislation go through the stages of a bill then signing into law. This is called delegated legislation. Delegated legislation means that bodies (i.e. Government agencies, Minister for Health, Minister for Transport etc) can make new law with to implement the requirements of legislation with the relevant authority.

---

[50] IBID

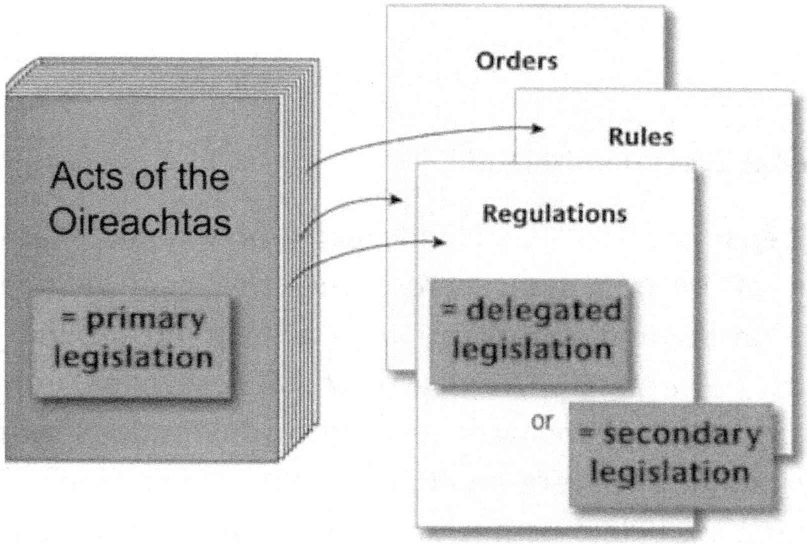

Secondary legislation, in the form of Statutory Instruments, is governed by the ***Statutory Instruments Act 1947***.[51] There are five main types of statutory instrument orders, regulations, rules, bye-laws and schemes. Secondary legislation was issued in the form of Statutory Rules and Orders between 1922 and 1947. Delegated legislation is a practical way to avoid overloading the Oireachtas.

[51] Statutory Instruments Act, 1947 http://www.irishstatutebook.ie/1947/en/act/pub/0044/

Chapter Five

Penology

The Early Penal System in Ireland

The early penal system in Ireland really only took shape after the introduction of incarceration, before the 18th century goals (prisons where those on remand were kept) were a dumping ground for debtors and vagrants. ***The Irish Prisons Act of 1826*** saw the introduction of Bridewells, until then there were few reform institutions as punishment was usually capital or severe enough to deter future criminal behaviour. Cesare Baccaria's article on crime and punishment was published in 1864 after this the Irish Penal System started to improve slowly, there was the introduction of Bridewells (petty offender prisons), this happened when the prison reformer John Howard made a trip to Ireland, here he noted the corruption in the Irish Prison Service.

A plethora of prisons or goals were built in the 19th century and many were designed and built to Jeremy Bentham's design. This was a circular guards hall with arms surrounding, this mean that guards could see all prisoners at all times. Mountjoy was built on this design. Kilmainham goal was built in 1789 and closed in 1910, this prison held many of the rebels from the 1916 Easter rising which saw them executed in the disused prison in May 1916. These prisons saw a great increase in times of Marshall law such as 1798 and 1804 and such times as there was outbreaks and ward of Independence.

Prisons were normally places where people were sent to reform, to retribution and punishment, however the 19th century saw a new prison, Grangegorman, this was a woman's prison, it was not based on punishment, it was based on moral reforming, unlike modern prisons there was segregation of prisoners, those who were convicted of minor or petty offences and those convicted of major offences, the authorities were careful not to allow the petty interact with the major criminals, this was to stop the petty thieves being influenced by the major criminals, it was used in the late 19th Century when prisoners were sent there while awaiting deportation. Prisons in Ireland held prisoners from all walks of life and sentences for theft, prostitution, drunk and disorderly behaviour and vagrancy were the most common, even offences life swearing warranted a prison sentence for some.

Ireland saw an huge increase in the prison population in the mid 1800's this was due to the great famine, many people committed offences which would see them incarcerated, this was better than going hungry or even dying from hunger. Many prisoners who committed petty crimes around this time were sent to Spike Island in Cork and then transported to Tasmania (of the coast of Australia) to serve their sentences; it was rare for any convict to return to Ireland after serving their transportation sentences.

Sentencing and Crime

Sentencing in Ireland, like many other common law Countries is decided by Judges, there are many mandatory sentences such as the sentencing for murder being life, this however gives the minister for justice the power to review the offender for parole after 8 years on the advice of the Parole Board of Ireland. Where an inmate is refused parole at 8 years they will be eligible again after 10 years to have their sentences reviewed again. Where there is not a mandatory sentence a judge uses what is called judicial discretion in sentencing.

Sentences should be just and fair, a sentence should reflect the seriousness of the crime and also the deterrence of further offences. This is often called the principle of proportionality; the sentence fits the crime, just as it is what is deserved and fair insofar as all that come before the court (rich or poor, black or white) should receive the same sentence.

When a judge is deciding the sentence for any case they may use mitigating factors or aggravating factors to lower the sentence from the allocated "maximum" sentence,

Once the seriousness of the offence is determined, the Judge will consider the various mitigating factors and aggravating factors which will determine the appropriate sentence.

A judge can only sentence an offender within their jurisdiction (authority over certain persons or areas), i.e. district court can sentence up to 12 months for one offence and 24 months for two or more offences, and they have the jurisdiction for offences which were committed in the jurisdiction, or where the offender resides or where the offender was arrested.

There are some factors which are considered in determining the length of the sentence such as;

- Did the accused person plead guilty or not guilty to the offence;(Mitigating Factor)
- Did they co-operate with the Gardaí; (Mitigating Factor)
- What were the circumstances of the crime, the facts of the case?
- Are there any aggravating factors in relation to the offence - was violent behaviour used; (Aggravating Factor)
- Has the accused person expressed regret for what they have done? (Mitigating Factor)
- Is the Accused a person of good character or have they previous convictions? (Mitigating Factor)
- The Judge will also consider the accused age, family circumstances, employment status, their health and any addictions they may have.

The judge will then consider the impact the offence had on the victim;

Judicial discretion also extends to the type of sentence, either a concurrent (all served together, i.e. two years for robbery, two years for trespass, suspect gets two years) or consecutive (All served one after the other, i.e. two years for robbery and two years for trespass, serve four years) sentence when deciding on the appropriate sentence of a person who is convicted of more than one offence. If a person receives a concurrent prison sentence, then that person is allowed to serve all of the sentences simultaneously. However, where the accused has committed an offence while on bail they will be sentenced consecutive to the original sentence.

Another discretion that a judge has is to suspend the sentence of the accused, some or all of the sentence may be suspended.

This power was given statutory power by the Criminal Justice Act 2006, this also gave judges the power to impose conditions on the offender such as good behaviour and restriction on entering certain areas or establishments etc. If the offender breaches these conditions their sentence can then be invoked.

It can be seen that judges in Ireland have wide discretionary powers, they are not limitless as seen in the previous page they must still act within the powers conferred on them in their jurisdiction, any decisions beyond the powers conferred on them are subject to judicial review (acting ultra vires "beyond powers allowed" and could be void), they must also give mandatory sentences for murder etc, there is no discretion in sentencing for murder.

The purpose of Prisons

Prisons take away liberty and freedom, so the main purpose of prison is punishment, the punishment continues inside prison (although technically not supposed to) as inmates are searched, etc in their cells and person, high use of CCTV, visit monitoring, and reading personal inmates correspondence etc.

It has often been said that the prison system is as much for society as for rehabilitation and punishment, i.e. people sleep better knowing that a criminal is off the street and cannot commit crimes against society while in there, Criminologists are often of the opinion that rehabilitation and education are better at reducing crime than prison sentences or "custodial sentences". There are many prisoners who continue to commit crimes while incarcerated and often involved in gang violence, others are often victims of abuse such as drug abuse and sexual assaults.

Alternatives to Prison Sentences

Suspended Sentences

Suspended sentences are normally having conditions attached. The judge has the discretion to suspend all or part of a sentence and attach conditions such as staying out of a certain area of the city or country, to stay away from a certain person, to undertake drug treatment or attend probationary meeting, breaching these orders may end up with the offender being sent back to finish the original sentence, however this I sat the discretion of the judge.

Community Service Orders

Community service orders are orders that order the offender to carry out voluntary or community work, such as rubbish clearing, horticulture assignments, flowerbeds and also cleaning of canals or rivers, these orders are given in conjunction with the Probation Service.

These orders can be given to those over 16, the order is for no less than 40 hours and no more than 240 hours, and this is a consent order , meaning the offender must agree. Orders are given under ***the Criminal Justice (Community Service) Act 1983.***

Probation Orders

These are given instead of custody or partial custody, (suspended all or part of the sentence) where the judge believes that the offender will abide by the terms, the terms of the orders are usually an undertaking that the offender will be of good behaviour, or enter treatment programmes, for drugs, alcohol or anger issues.

Restorative justice

This is new to Ireland, this is a sentence whereby the offender makes amends to the victim, they try to "fix" the wrong that was done, aplogoies or even meeting to discuss the offence and how they may compensate the victim for the wrong done to them, this is not about punishing the offender, its about allowing the victim a say and also meet with the offender to let them know the impact their crimes had on them.

The Modern Prison Service

Political responsibility for the Prison System in Ireland is vested in the Minister for Justice and Equality. The Irish Prison Service operates as an executive agency within the Department of Justice and Equality. It is headed by a Director General supported by 7 Directors. The Irish Prison Service is administered centrally with its headquarters located at IDA Business Park, Ballinalee Road, Longford, Co. Longford

The Prison Service operates within a statutory framework comprising:

(i) the Prisons Acts, including the most recent ***Prisons Act 2007,***

(ii) relevant provisions in other statutes such as ***the Prisons (Visiting Committees) Act, 1925, the Criminal Justice Act, 1960, the Criminal Justice (Miscellaneous Provisions) Act, 1997, the Criminal Justice Act, 2007, other criminal justice acts and the Transfer of Sentenced Persons Acts, 1995 and 1997*** and

(iii) ***the Rules for the Government of Prisons, 2007.***

For persons held on immigration related matters the main legislative provisions are the Immigration Acts 1999, 2003 and 2004, their associated regulations, the Illegal Immigrants Trafficking Act 2000 and the Refugee Act 1996.

The Prison Service also takes due account of the UN and European Conventions on Human Rights, UN Standard Minimum Rules for the Treatment of Prisoners, the UN Convention against Torture and other Cruel, Inhuman or Degrading Treatment or Punishment, the UN Covenant on Civil and Political Rights, the European Convention for the Prevention of Torture and Inhuman or Degrading Treatment or Punishment.

Location of Prisons and Places of Detention

Ireland's Prisons

There are 14 institutions in the Irish Prison System consisting of 11 traditional "closed" institutions, two open centres which operate with minimal internal and perimeter security, and one “semi-open" facility with traditional perimeter security but minimal internal security (the Training Unit). The majority of female prisoners are accommodated in the purpose-built "Dóchas Centre" and the remainder are located in a separate part of Limerick Prison.

Mountjoy: Committal prison for adult male prisoners, at North Circular Road, Dublin 7.

Dóchas: Committal prison for female prisoners aged

17 years and over at North Circular Road, Dublin 7

Limerick: Committal prison for adult male and female, at Mulgrave Street, Limerick.

Cork: Committal prison for adult male prisoners, at Rathmore Road, Cork.

Castlerea: Committal prison for adult male prisoners, at Harristown, Castlerea, Co. Roscommon.

Cloverhill: Committal prison for remand adult male prisoners, at Cloverhill Road, Clondalkin, Dublin 22

Arbour Hill: Prison for adult male prisoners, at Arbour Hill, Dublin 7.

Midlands: Prison for adult male prisoners, at Dublin Road, Portlaoise, Co. Laois.

Portlaoise: Prison for adult male prisoners, including the detention of high security prisoners, at Dublin Road, Portlaoise, Co. Laois

Wheatfield : Prison for adult male prisoners, at Cloverhill Road, Clondalkin.

Shelton Abbey: An open centre for male prisoners aged 19 years and over,at Arklow, Co. Wicklow

St. Patricks Institution: An institution for male juveniles aged 16 to 21 years, at North Circular Road, Dublin 7.

Loughan House: An open centre for the detention of male prisoners aged 18 years and over, at Blacklion, Co. Cavan

Training Unit: A semi-open place of detention for male prisoners aged 18 years and over, at Glengarriff Parade, Dublin 7, for industrial training.

Probation Service and the Irish Criminal Justice System

The Role of the Probation Service within the Irish Criminal Justice System

The Probation Service is an agency of the Department of Justice and Equality. The Probation Service are sometimes involved in the Criminal Justice Process between the prosecution and trial phase, for example when a court requires a Probation Officer to hold a family conference. More often, the Probation Service become involved in the criminal justice process between the trial and sanction phases, often in cases where a trial court requires a pre-sanction assessment and report to assist in deciding on an appropriate sanction. In some cases, the court may be considering placing an offender on probation supervision or community service.

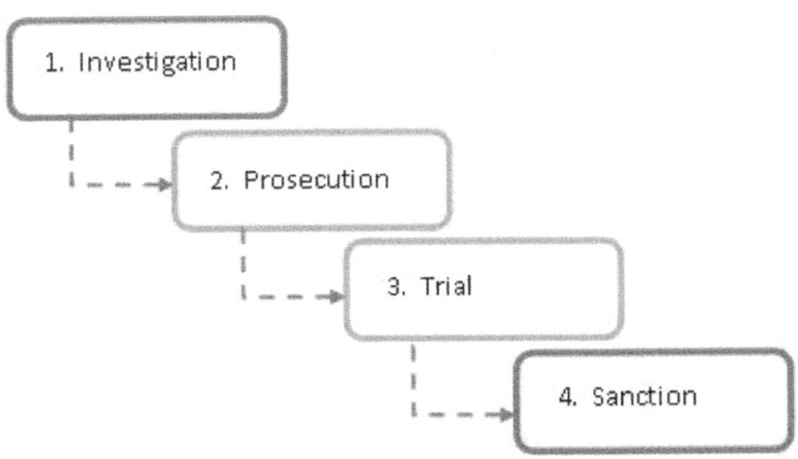

Where the court decides on a community-based sanction, The Probation Service is responsible for managing the sanction and supervising the offender. They help offenders to become better citizens and make good the harm done by crime. The Probation Service also undertakes whatever steps are appropriate to reduce the risk of future harm or re-offending by the offender.

The Probation Service has an important role in planning and preparing for the release of prisoners and their return to the community. They also supervise some offenders after their release from prison. This particular role is focused on reintegrating the offender in society, with the priority of protecting the public and reducing the risk of re-offending. The Probation Service works closely with the other agencies of the criminal justice system, as illustrated in the diagram below, to reduce crime and make communities safer.

The Probation Service co-operates with criminal justice agencies in other jurisdictions, especially in cases where offenders move between countries.

The Garda Siochána

History of the Gardai

An Garda Síochána was formed in 1922, until this time policing was the job of the Royal Irish Constabulary (RIC) and Dublin Metropolitan Police.

After the signing of the Anglo Irish Treaty the new state would not allow the RIC to continue due to its British roots and loyalties, the Metro continued until 1925when it was amalgamated with the Gardai.

The Civic Guards

The push to recruit new garda had at its heart new rules, members had to be single, over 5 feet 9 and be able to read write and pass maths. The first Commissioner of the new Garda force was Michael Staines. This first garda were somewhat of a failure, while training in the military barracks in Kildare over 1000 new gardai broke ranks and stormed the armoury. This mutiny continued for over seven weeks and talks were exhaustive it was finally ended when Michael Collins took over the talks. Staines resigned amid claims that those opposed to the treaty were the main cause of the mutiny. By the end of 1922 the guards were stationed throughout the Country, the transference was somewhat peaceful, however this peace was shattered when a barracks accident led to the death of a young guards, it was after this time that arms were removed from the guards and they became arms free.

Criminal division of the Gardai

It was on the same day as Michael Collins was shot on the 22nd August 1922 that the criminal division was established. This was separate to the civil guards and was formed from members of the Irish Republican Police and members of the Army. It consisted of over 100 heavily armed men and three women who posed as typists but whose real job was to ferret out women engaged in anti-state activities.

By October 1923 the Free State was stable enough for the CID to be disbanded and its personnel transferred to the Dublin Metropolitan Police, by 1925 the DMP and CID were amalgamated with the Garda Síochána

Modern Gardai

The Mission of An Garda Síochána is

Working with Communities to Protect and Serve.

An Garda Siochana is a community based organisation with more than 15,000 Garda and civilian employees.

These include...

- Air Support Unit
- Ballistics Unit
- Mounted Unit
- Technical Support Services
- Water Unit
- National Bureau of Fraud Investigation
- Fingerprint Unit
- Photographic Unit National
- Drugs Unit

- Mapping Unit
- National Immigration Unit

There are other criminal divisions of the gardai

Criminal Arrests

As defined in the ***CRIMINAL JUSTICE ACT 1984*** *and* ***CRIMINAL ASSETS BUREAU ACT 1996***

The Criminal Justice Act, 1984

Reinforced the powers of the Gardaí in their detention of suspects · It also protected the rights of those suspects being detained in Garda custody The first legislative power to detain a suspect was contained in ***the Offences against the State Act 1939***.

Section 30 of The Criminal Justice Act of 1984 contained a statutory power to detain any suspect at a Garda station for questioning following their arrest, it authorises any member to detain a suspect following arrest for a period of 24 hours. A person may then be detained for a further period of 24 hours if such detention is authorised by a member not below the rank of Superintendent.

The power of detention in the ***Section 4 of The Criminal Justice Act of 1984*** is normally invoked when detaining suspects at garda stations for further questioning. ***Sections*** *4(1) and 4(2)* states that the offence must be serious (indictable) , i.e. it must carry a possible sentence of over five years such as murder, assault causing harm, sexual offences, theft, etc. ***Sections*** *4(1) and 4(2)* stated that there must be reasonable cause for the arrest and the detention must be necessary for a proper investigation of the offence. These conditions must be satisfied in order for the arrest and detention to be lawful under ***Section 4 of the of The Criminal Justice Act of 1984.***

If those rules are not adhered to then a principle called the "*Fruit of the poison tree*": occurs, this means that if the arrest/detention is unlawful, any evidence arising from unlawfulness may not be used in the trial against the suspect.

The suspect's detention is timed from their arrest (not the time they arrive at the Garda station), this time starts of as six hours, again from the time of arrest, whereby the senior garda must be advised of the nature of the crime, facts and evidence to date, any further enquiries needed, the garda, not below Superintendent then decides if the suspect can be detained further. Between the hours of midnight to 8am the suspect can request the questioning be suspended and resumed at 8am. They are also entitled to rest periods, however they can waive those rights but this must be signed by the suspect.

Under Section5 of The Criminal Justice Act of 1984 states that a suspect is entitled to access to a solicitor. Their next of kin must also be notified. If a suspect is denied any of these rights their conviction may be overturned. *DPP V Healy*

Section 6 of The Criminal Justice Act of 1984 deals with the powers available to the Gardaí in relation to someone in custody, such as taking their name, addresses, fingerprints etc. Gardai have the powers to demand a suspect name, and address, search their person, take any swabs or fingerprints required and even skin samples, if the suspect is suspected of handling firearms or explosives. Finally, take and seize any property or possession of the suspect in relation to the investigation.

Section 7 of The Criminal Justice Act of 1984, this section was introduced to give effect to the Treatment of Persons in Custody Regulations.

They rules are set out on a sheet which is handed to the suspect on his arrival at the station, and he is asked to sign the custody record to indicate receipt of a copy of his rights, however by ***Subsection 3*** of this Section states that non-occurrence of these right may not necessarily overturn the custody. As set out in ***Section 4***, only a serious breach can overturn the custody.

Criminal Assets Bureau (CAB)

As defined in the ***CRIMINAL ASSETS BUREAU ACT 1996***

The Criminal Assets Bureau Act, or CAB Act is believed to be one of the foremost and progressive pieces of legislation to emerge from Ireland or the EU for that fact. This piece of legislation was enacted after the murder of Gerry McCabe and Veronica Guerin in 1996, by gangland criminals. This legislation was introduced to curb the almost limitless power of gangland and drugs lords in Ireland, it means that whereby any proceeds of crime or proceeds from gangland or affiliation to them, drug dealers or criminals homes, bank accounts and private property could be seized, in essence the place where it hurt most. Until the enactment of this piece of legislation criminals could use the constitutional right to home and private property in their advantage and make it unconstitutional to take any of it, hence, allowing them to keep for themselves or their families the proceeds of their crimes. Alongside the CAB Act the Bails Act 1997 was introduced, this piece of legislation allowed the courts to refuse bail if they were of the belief that an accused person would commit further offences while on bail. A far cry from the old Bail Act, which stated the accused, could be denied bail if there was a reasonable belief that they would interfere with a witness or not attend their hearing, this new, no longer was the presumption of innocence in the forefront, but in essence the presumption of guilt..!!

In its first ten years in operation, CAB collected €89 million in illegal assets. As of 2016 it continues to be one of the most effective and dynamic pieces of legislation to deal with criminals and the proceeds of their crimes.

Special Detective Unit

The Special Detective Unit (SDU) is part of the Crime and Security branch and holds primary responsibility for State security.

Security and Intelligence Branch

The Security and Intelligence Branch was formed to counter the threat posed by domestic and international terrorist groups.

Domestic Violence Sexual Assault Investigation Unit

Domestic Violence Sexual Assault Investigation Unit is responsible for the Investigation of Sexual Crimes, Crimes against Children and Child Welfare. The Sex Offender Management and Intelligence Unit also works under this branch, it is responsible for maintaining a record of all persons who are subject to the requirements of the Sex Offenders Act 2001.

Along with the Air Support Teams, Community Policing and Mounted Units the Irish Gardai is amongst the most progressive in the modern world and successful integration of community with a fair and just Policing of the Irish State.

The functions of the Gardai

The Gardai are responsible for making sure that the law of the State is obeyed and that those who do not obey the law are arrested and brought before the courts. *Gardai is the Irish word for "guardians". An Gardai Siochana means "guardians of the peace".* The primary function of An Garda Síochána is to ensure that people feel safe on the streets and in their homes. Building stronger and safer communities contributes greatly to improving the quality of life for the people.

The function of An Garda Síochána is to serve the community by implementing and upholding the law as legislated by Government. With the participation and dedication of the Gardaí, other community stakeholders (e.g. retail outlets, public services, public amenities) are, as far as possible, ensured of safety and they in turn commit to law abidance to serve the common good of the community. To ensure a positive strategy, issues such as the quality of the service provided and the strength and commitment of the partnerships amongst service providers and citizens must be ensured.

The Gardaí make a commitment to the community they serve, to provide:

- a good quality service,
- an open and transparent force which is accountable for its actions,
- the equal provision of services towards all members of the community who access the service or come into contact with the force,
- consultation and information to the local community on issues that impact them or may do so in the future and
- support to the local community activities by playing an active role.

The Court System in Ireland

The Petty Sessions

These were the courts of the lands, these courts dealt with both civil ad criminal cases, however they are nothing like our modern courts, these courts in summary offences (relatively minor) had no judge, just a Justice of the Peace, this JoP was not legally qualified, usually a prominent member of the community whose decisions were final. However, if there were serious or indictable (needing a jury) there were held four times per year, these were called quarterly sessions, and presided over by a Judge and jury. More serious offences were dealt with at assizes (hearings) on twice yearly basis, these were a two tier case, there was two juries, one (the grand) would hear if there was a case on legal fact, and the other trial jury which would decide the offenders guilt or innocence. Prisoners who were arrested between assizes were held on remand in goals such as Kilmainham and Grangegorman.

Superior Courts in Ireland (pre 1900)

Pre 1900 Ireland had several superior courts, the oldest and most significant were the Courts of Chancery, King's or Queen's Bench, Common Pleas and Exchequer which was renamed the Four Courts in 1877. These courts dealt predominately with administrative cases but it also dealt with legal matters. A Clerk of the Crown and Peace in each county maintained the records for each court.

The transition from the assizes to the modern system took place from 1900 to 1920; this was changed in 1920s with the introduction of the Dáil courts and the ordinary court system. This system was fraught with difficulty. The District Court replaced the Petty Sessions; the new Circuit

Court was held in four districts and replaced the County courts, this system stayed until the introduction of the modern Court System.

The Supreme Court and court of Criminal Appeal

Both of these courts were established in 1924 under the Courts of Justice Act, 1924, which was given its powers by the Irish Free State (Constitution) Act, 1922, which was on foot of the Anglo Irish Treaty in 1921.[52]

---

52 http://www.courts.ie/Courts.ie/Library3.nsf/pagecurrent/8B9125171CFBA78080256DE5004011F8

The Modern Court System in Ireland

The Function of the Courts

The courts system in Ireland has its historic origins in the British Courts System that was in use in Ireland up to 1922. The 1922 Constitution was enacted on the foundation of the Irish Free State. That Constitution provided for the setting up of new courts to replace the existing Courts that had evolved under the British administration. ***The Courts of Justice Act, 1924*** established the legal basis for a new Court system.

Ireland has a written Constitution and Articles 34 to 37 of the Constitution deal with the administration of justice in general. Article 34.1 states that 'Justice shall be administered in Courts established by law'.

The Constitution outlines the structure of the court system as comprising:

- A court of final appeal, known as the Supreme Court,
- Courts of first instance which include the High Court with full jurisdiction in all criminal and civil matters and
- Courts of limited jurisdiction including
- the Circuit Court and the
- District Court organised on a regional basis.

The present courts were set up by ***the Courts (Establishment and Constitution) Act 1961*** pursuant to Article 34 of the Constitution adopted by the Irish people in 1937. We are concerned mainly with the courts as they are relevant to personal injury and property litigation and we have focused on this area in the linked pages attached.

The Courts Act 2004 contains much that is relevant to the day-to-day handling of Personal Injury Claims within the Courts System.

- District Court
- Circuit Court
- High Court
- Central Criminal Court
- Appeal Court
- Supreme Court

The Irish Court system was established under Articles 64 to 73 of the Irish Constitution enacted in 1922. ***The Courts of Justice Act 1924*** set out the structure and Hierarchy of the Irish Courts and the final structure of the Irish Courts was set out in the Irish Constitution of 1937 under Articles 34 to 38, there was a Constitutional challenge to the structure and hierarch of the Court set out in the 1937 Constitution, this challenge case *"The State (Killian) v Minister for Justice [1954]"*[53] found that new legislation was required to re-establish the hierarchy and structure of the Courts. This legislation came in the form of ***the Courts (Establishment and Constitution) Act 1961 and the Courts (Supplemental Provisions) Act 1961.***

Article 34 of the Irish Constitution states that: *"Justice shall be administered in courts established by law by Judges appointed in the manner provided by this Constitution"*[54] *"justice will be administered by*

---

[53] The State (Killian) v Minister for Justice [1954] IR 207

[54]http://www.supremecourt.ie/supremecourt/sclibrary3.nsf/pagecurrent/D5F78352A387D744802573150 05A419E?opendocument&l=en

courts established by law and justice should generally be administered in public". This does not cover family law

Article 38 of the Irish Constitution states that 'no person shall be tried on any criminal charge save in the due course of law'.

The Irish Court system is hierarchical in nature with the Supreme Court being the highest, followed by the High Court, the Circuit Court, and the District Court. The Employment Appeals Tribunal, An Bord Pleanála, and the Labour Court are in the administrative divisions and deal with specialised areas of the law.

The superiority of Supreme Court judges was set out in ***the Courts of Justice Act 1924*** and confirmed by ***the Courts Act 1997.***

The Hierarchy of the Courts, starting with the inferior courts are as follow:

The District Court in Ireland

The District Court is the lowest court in the court system; the District Court was established in 1961. ***The Courts and Court Officers (Amendment) Act 2007*** the numbers of judges should not be more than 60, excluding the President of the Court, however this has since been extended to 63. The currently President is Judge Rosemary Horgan.

There are 24 Districts in Ireland, including the Dublin Metropolitan District, each with its own court being presided over by a judge sitting alone (that is, one judge, no jury).

Function & Jurisdiction

The District Court hears civil and criminal which are relatively minor. The District Court hear cases which are Summary in nature

District Criminal Court

In criminal matters, its jurisdiction is limited to cases which a judge sits alone, (there is no jury) the maximum penalty is 12 months' imprisonment for one offence or 24 months for two or more offences. Again, the maximum penalty is 12 months' imprisonment for one offence or 24 months for two or more offences. Cases in the District Court are those that are non-jury trials of minor offences which include most road traffic offences, TV licensing offences and parking fines, these are called Summary (or less serious) offences.

There are some Indictable (more serious) cases that cannot be heard in the District Court, including, rape, treason, murder, aggravated sexual assault, and piracy, which can never be heard in the District Court and must be referred up to the Circuit Court or the Central Criminal Court.

In respect of offences, the District Court Judge will be presented with the Book of Evidence, the prosecution and defence will present their submissions including bail applications, before deciding whether there is a sufficient case to answer. If so, the accused will the sent forward for trial to the Circuit Court or the Central Criminal Court, depending on the severity of the offence.

Appeals

There are, essentially, two types of appeal: a *de novo* appeal, and an appeal on a point of law.

De novo

When a *de novo* appeal is granted it means that the case is completely re-heard from the beginning by a higher court. For District Court cases, all *de novo* appeals are heard by the Circuit Court. The Circuit Court's determination is final and cannot be appealed.

On a point of law

These are heard by the High Court, and can occur either during the case (referred to as a "consultative case stated") or after the case has been heard in full (referred to as "an appeal by way of case stated"). In such appeals, the High Court is only concerned with the legal issues and not in the findings of the District Court.

An example of this would be where there was some confusion as to the meaning of a particular law (legislation). If this was the case, the matter could be sent to the High Court to clear up any ambiguity. Once the matter is cleared up it is sent back to the District Court so that the case may continue, or so that any relevant changes can be made to the ruling.

Judicial review

While not strictly an appeal, there is also a remedy called ***judicial review.*** In the District Court, this means that, where an individual is of the belief that a judge or other government agency has acted in excess of its jurisdiction (***Ultra Virus***) or contrary to its duty, that person can query or challenge that action in the High Court.

The Circuit Court in Ireland

Under *the Court and Court Officers (Amendment) Act 2007* the Circuit Court comprises of 37 ordinary judges and is presided over by Mr. Justice Raymond Groarke.

There are 8 Circuits in Ireland - Dublin, Cork, Eastern, South Eastern, Western, South Western, Northern, and Midlands. Dublin and Cork are the only permanent courts throughout the year. There are 10 judges assigned to the Dublin Circuit Court, and 3 to the Cork Circuit Court, the rest are divided between the remaining Circuit Courts. It also acts as an appeal court from the District Court. In criminal cases the Circuit Court is presided over by a judge sitting with a jury of twelve persons. In civil cases the Court is presided over by a judge sitting alone.

Function & Jurisdiction of the Circuit Court

The Circuit Court hears civil and criminal cases in a variety of matters which also include de novo appeals from the District Court. The Circuit Court covers indictable offences and has a jury

Structure of the Circuit Criminal Court

The Circuit Court has a wide jurisdiction in respect of criminal matters. It deals with all indictable offences which are sent forward from the District Court, however there are some exceptions, including rape, murder, aggravated sexual assault, treason, and piracy. These cases must be heard in the Central Criminal Court.

Appeals

Apart from hearing appeals from the District Court, the Circuit Court can also hear appeals from decisions of the Labour Court, the Unfair Dismissals Tribunal, and the Employment Appeals Tribunal.

There are in essence two types of appeal available to those whose judgements are in the Circuit Court: a *de novo* appeal, and an appeal on a point of law.

De novo

When a *de novo* appeal is granted it means that the case is completely re-heard from the beginning by a higher court. For District Court cases, all *de novo* appeals are heard by the High Court. For criminal cases, all *de novo* appeals are heard by the Court of Criminal Appeal. Determinations of the High Court and the Court of Criminal Appeal are final and cannot be appealed.

On a point of law

These are heard by the High Court, and can occur either during the case (referred to as a "consultative case stated") or after the case has been heard in full (referred to as "an appeal by way of case stated"). In such appeals, the High Court is only concerned with the legal issues and not in the findings of the Circuit Court.

An example of this would be where there was some confusion as to the meaning of a particular law (legislation). If this was the case, the matter could be sent to the High Court to clear up any ambiguity. Once the matter is cleared up it is sent back to the Circuit Court so that the case may continue, or so that any relevant changes can be made to the ruling.

Judicial review

While not strictly an appeal, there is also a remedy called ***judicial review.*** In the Circuit Court, this means that, where an individual is of the belief that a judge or other government agency has acted in excess of its jurisdiction (***Ultra Virus***) or contrary to its duty, that person can query or challenge that action in the High Court.

The High Court in Ireland

The High Court of Ireland has full original jurisdiction the power "to determine all matters and questions whether of law or fact, civil or criminal". It can decide the validity of any law, having regard to the provisions of the Constitution and hear murder and rape trials though under ***Competition Act, 2002*** and associated cases or cases that results from it.

Structure of the High Court of Ireland

The High Court is presided over by the Honourable Mr. Justice Nicholas Kearns and 36 ordinary judges. In Civil cases one judge sitting alone usually presides over the proceedings, but in some cases of defamation, assault and battery, false imprisonment, and malicious prosecution all require a jury. There are times for instance when there is a case of national importance i.e. the constitutionality of a new bill, the High Court will sit with three judges. The High Court hears appeals from the Circuit Court in civil cases. There are no juries per se in civil cases in the High Court with one exception; this exception is in libel cases where the case will be decided by a judge and jury.

The High Court is based in Dublin but a division of the High Court sits in several provincial locations such as Cork, Galway, Limerick, Waterford, Sligo, Dundalk, Kilkenny and Ennis at specified times during the year to deal with personal injury cases and appeals from the various Circuit Courts in civil and family law matters.

Structure of the High Court (Central Criminal Court) of Ireland

Where criminal matters are concerned, the High Court is referred to as the Central Criminal Court, or the Criminal Court area of the High Court. This court only hears cases of a more serious nature which the lower courts cannot deal with lower courts. Examples include murder, rape, aggravated sexual assault, treason, and piracy.

Appeals in the High Court (criminal division) of Ireland

An appeal from the High Court in civil cases can only go to the Supreme Court on foot of permission which is applied for under the "leapfrog appeal" system, however all other appeals go to the Court of Appeal..

The Special Criminal Court in Ireland

Deals with:

- treason
- encouragement or concealing knowledge of treason
- offences relating to the obstruction of government and obstruction of the President
- murder, attempted murder, conspiracy to murder
- piracy
- offences under the Genocide Act, 1973
- rape, aggravated sexual assault and attempted aggravated sexual assault under the Criminal Law (Rape) (Amendment) Act, 1990

The Special Criminal Court was set up under ***the Offences against the State Act 1939*** and sits with no jury. The cases it can deal with are limited and usually Terrorism or Gangland.

There is no Jury in this court and is presided over by three judges, these three judges are taken from a pool of 11 judges which are chosen from the High, Circuit and District Courts. Appeals from the Special Criminal Court against conviction or sentence are taken to the Court of Appeal.

The Court of Appeal in Ireland

The Court of Appeal, came into existence on 28th October 2014, it was established by the *Court of Appeal Act 2014,* the Court of Appeal which sits between the High Court and the Supreme Court.

The Court of Appeal is composed of a President and nine ordinary judges. The Chief Justice and the President of the High Court (The Honourable Mr Justice Sean Ryan) in addition to the President, the Court will comprise nine ordinary judges. Six High Court judges have been nominated for appointment to the Court, namely Mr Justice Peter Kelly, Ms Justice Mary Finlay Geoghegan, Mr Justice George Birmingham, Ms Justice Mary Irvine, Mr Justice Gerard Hogan, and, Mr Justice Michael Peart. The remaining three positions have yet to be filled by the Judicial Appointments Advisory Board.

Some interlocutory and procedural applications may be heard by the President alone or by another judge nominated by the President. The Court of Appeal will be an automatic appeal court from the High

Appeals in criminal proceedings

Under *the Court of Appeal Act 2014*, the Court of Appeal was given the appellate jurisdiction previously exercised by the Court of Criminal Appeal.

Criminal Appeals from the Circuit Court or Central Criminal Court who require a certificate from the trial judge that the case is a fit one for appeal now lie to the Court of Appeal. If this certificate is refused, the Court of Appeal itself, on appeal from this refusal, can grant leave to appeal. In addition, the Director of Public Prosecutions may appeal a sentence on grounds of alleged undue leniency under section 2 of the *Criminal Justice Act 1993*. An alleged case under miscarriage of justice, an appeal can be lodged under section 2 of the ***Criminal Procedure Act 1993***. [55]

The Court of Appeal was also given jurisdiction to hear appeals by the Director of Public Prosecutions on a question of law arising out of criminal trials which resulted in an acquittal. The decision of the Court of Appeal does not affect the acquittal verdict in such cases.

Appeals by the Director of Public Prosecutions against an acquittal or against a decision not to order a retrial also lie to the Court of Appeal.

---

[55]http://www.courts.ie/Courts.ie/library3.nsf/pagecurrent/5E9C21E72309A7D280257D7F0045A86A?opendocument

The Supreme Court in Ireland

The Supreme Court sits in the Four Courts in Dublin and is the highest court in the system. It consists of the President or the Chief Justice, her Honour Ms. Justice Susan Denham and 7 ordinary judges. Under ***section.5 of the Courts (No. 2) Act 1997***, the number of judges may also be exceeded by one where a former Chief Justice serves as a judge of the Supreme Court. The Court hears appeals from the High Court and the Court of Appeal. The Court has the power to decide if the provisions of any statute are repugnant to the Constitution should the President refer such provisions to the Court prior to the statute being enacted. Under ***Article 26 of the Irish Constitution 1937*** the President has the power to send a Bill to the Supreme Court to test its constitutionality before signing it into law

In procedural matters or minor cases, three judges sit. For matters involving a constitutional challenge to a statute, or where an important question of law arises, five judge's sit, the Supreme Court can be requested to review a Bill referred to it by the President as to whether or not such a Bill is repugnant to the Constitution, if this event takes place then seven judges sit. Where there are applications for the appointment of Notaries Public and Commissioners for Oaths, or for case management lists the Chief Justice can sit alone.

Appeals

The main day-to-day business of the Supreme Court is to hear appeals from the Court of Appeal, or from the High Court ("leapfrog" appeals under limited circumstances "see high court notes").

The Supreme Court does not hear the evidence of witnesses as there is no witness box in the Supreme Court. Appeals are heard on the basis of the documents that were before the original court and a transcript of the oral evidence that was given in the original court and, where the trial judge approves them, legal counsels' notes of the evidence.

Decisions of Judges in the Supreme Court

Decisions are made based on a majority ruling, though each judge is entitled to deliver a separate judgement, regardless of whether or not it agrees with the majority ruling. There are two exceptions to this - where deciding on the validity of a law or on the constitutionality or otherwise of a Bill, the majority decision is the only one pronounced.

These decisions are sometimes given ex tempore (immediately). There are times however when Judges reserve the right to reserve its decision pending consideration of the facts whereby they will deliver their decision at a future date.

Personnel involved in the court room

The Judge

The judge is in charge of court proceedings and decides any legal issues arising in the case.

The Registrar / Court Clerk

The registrar / court clerk assists the judge with administrative matters and is in charge of the court documents and exhibits. He/she also records the names of witnesses and the decision in the case. The registrar / court clerk also administers the oath.

Solicitor

Solicitors meet with clients and get instructions from them. They prepare the case for trial by getting all the papers ready and choosing/briefing a barrister to present the case.

The Jury

The jury hears the evidence and decides on the guilt or innocence of the accused in a criminal case and which party wins in a civil case.

The Court Reporter / Stenographer

The stenographer takes a note of everything said in the case and later types up the notes in the event of an appeal being lodged.

Witness

Witnesses are called by either party to prove their side of the story and may be cross-examined by the opposing party as to the accuracy of their evidence.

Counsel

The barristers in the case are known as counsel. They are hired by the solicitor to prosecute or defend the case in court.

DPP (criminal)

The Department of public prosecutions brings cases against the accused in criminal cases, they bring the case on behalf of the citizens.

Tipstaff / Judge's Usher

The tipstaff / judge's usher is the personal assistant to the judge. He/she walks ahead of the judge carrying a staff and says "all rise" as the judge enters the courtroom.

Defendant (criminal)

The accused comes before the court accused of a crime.

Defendant (civil)

The person being sued or the case is being brought against.

Plaintiff

The person bringing the civil case against another civilian or the state.

Prison Officer (Criminal)

Sits in attendance with the accused.

Public

Members of the general public are permitted in the public gallery, except in camera or family/child custody cases.

Civil Liability & Courts Act 2004

Many people involved in claims believe that over time this act has an even greater chance of revolutionising the overall scene. While no one has objection to reasonable compensation being paid to genuine claimants by those who are liable for their injuries, far too often many of these vital components were ignored. Added to this was the requirement to pay costs in far too many straightforward cases. PIAB is really more about that problem, The Courts Act begins to get to the heart of the matter.

Conclusion

The definition of crime is challenging because acts that are defined as criminal vary across time and cultures. Many criminologists believe that because crimes are over defined they cannot determine what real crimes are and criminals are.

This introductory guide was designed to give you a background in Criminology, if you would like to continue your criminology studies further I recommend the following books and publications as part of your academic or personal learning journey into the study, causation, and prevention of crime;

Recommended reading

Carrabine, E., Iganski, P., Lee, M., Plummer, K. and South, N. (2008) Criminology: A Sociological Introduction. London: Routledge.

Hale et al. [2013 ed.] Criminology [3rd ed.]. Oxford: Oxford UP.

Kilkelly, U [2006] Youth Justice in Ireland: Tough Lives, Rough justice. Sallins, Co. Kildare: Irish Academic Press.

Kilcommins, S[2004] Crime, punishment and the search for order in Ireland. Dublin: Institute of Public Administration.

Maguire, M. (ed) (2012) The Oxford Handbook of Criminology. Oxford: Oxford University Press

McLaughlin & John Muncie [2013] The Sage Dictionary of Criminology. [3rd ed.]. London: Sage.

Webber, C. (2010) Psychology and Crime. London: Sage

Bibliography

Bonger et al (1916) *Criminality and economic conditions,* Little, Brown, and Company, Boston

Briggs J. Harrison C. McInnes A. Vincent D. (2005) Crime and Punishment in England: An introductory History London: Routledge

Burke R.H. (2005) *An Introduction to Criminal Theory* Cullompton: Willan Publishing

Chesney-Lind, M., & Irwin, K. (2004). From badness to meanness: Popular constructions of contemporary girlhood. In A. Harris (Ed.), All about the girl: Culture, power, and identity (pp. 45-56). New York: Routledge.

Citizens Information. (2014). Supreme Court of Ireland. Retrieved May 2014, from Citizen Information: http://www.citizensinformation.ie/en/justice/courts_system/supreme_court.html

Clarke, R. V. and M. Felson (Eds.) (1993). Routine Activity and Rational Choice. Advances in Criminological Theory, Vol 5. New Brunswick, NJ: Transaction Books.

Cockburn J. S. (1977) Crime in England 1550-1800 London: Methuen & Co Ltd.

Courts Service. (2009). History of the state. Retrieved from Courts Service: http://www.courts.ie/Courts.ie/library3.nsf/pagecurrent/8B9125171CFBA78080256DE5004011F8?opendocument

Cunneen, C. and White, R. (2007) Juvenile Justice: Youth and Crime In Australia, Third Edition, Oxford University Press, Melbourne.

Department of Justice, Equality and Law Reform (2009) Fear of Crime in Ireland and its Impact on Quality of Life. Stationary Office. Dublin

Evans E.J. (1994) Sir Robert Peel London: Routledge.

Garland D. (1997) 'Of Crimes and Criminals: The Development of Criminology in Britain.

Graber, D. (1980). Crime News and the Public. New York: Praeger Publishers

Hirschi, T (1969) *Causes of Delinquency.* University of California Press.

Irish Statute Book. (2009). Criminal Justice (Public Order) Act, 1994. Retrieved 2012, from Irish Statute Book, : http://www.irishstatutebook.ie/eli/1994/act/2/section/8/enacted/en/html

Irish Statute Book. (2009). Criminal Justice (Public Order) Act, 1994. Retrieved 2011, from Irish Statute Book: http://www.irishstatutebook.ie/eli/1994/act/2/section/9/enacted/en/html

Irish Statute Book. (2010). Criminal Justice Act 2006. Retrieved 2012, from Irish Statute Book: http://www.irishstatutebook.ie/eli/2006/act/26/section/184/enacted/en/html

Irish Statute Book. (2014). Criminal Justice (Public Order) Act 2011. Retrieved 2014, from Irish Statute Book: http://www.irishstatutebook.ie/eli/2011/act/5/section/2/enacted/en/html

Irish Statute Book S14. (n.d.). Criminal Justice (Public Order) Act, 1994. Retrieved from Irish Statute Book: http://www.irishstatutebook.ie/eli/1994/act/2/section/14/enacted/en/html

Irish Statute Book S15. (2012). Section 15 of the Criminal Justice (Public Order) Act 1994 . Retrieved 2013, from Irish Statute Book: http://www.irishstatutebook.ie/eli/1994/act/2/section/15/enacted/en/html

Irish Statute Book S16. (2010). Criminal Justice (Public Order) Act, 1994. Retrieved 2012, from Irish Statute Book: http://www.irishstatutebook.ie/eli/1994/act/2/section/16/enacted/en/html

Irish Statute book, S. (2009). Criminal Justice Act (Public order) Act 1994. Retrieved 2011, from Irish Statute Book: http://www.irishstatutebook.ie/eli/1994/act/2/section/18/enacted/en/html

Klein D. (2004) The Etiology of Female Crime in McLaughlin E. Muncie J. Hughes G(Eds.) Criminological Perspectives (2nd Ed) London: Sage

Maguire M. Morgan R. Reiner R. (eds) *The Oxford Handbook of Criminology* Oxford: Oxford University Press.

McIntyre, McMullan and O Toghda, Criminal Law (Dublin, 2012)

McAuley and McCutcheon, Criminal liability: A Grammar (Dublin, 2000).

Nelken D. (1997) 'White Collar Crime' in Maguire M. Morgan R. Reiner R. (eds) The Oxford Handbook of Criminology Oxford: Oxford University Press

NI Shuinear, S. (2003); 'Irish Travellers: 'Ethnolect, Alliance, Control', (London), University of Greenwich

Siegel, Larry J. (2006) Criminology; 9th Edition. Thomson/Wadsworth, Belmont, CA.

Skogan, W. (1987). 'The Impact of Victimisation on Fear'. Crime and Delinquency 33(1): 135-154

Soothill, K. Peelo, M. Taylor, C. (2003) *Making Sense of Criminology.* Cambridge: Polity

The Brehon Laws. (2011). Retrieved April 2014, from Brehon Law: http://brehonlaw-justice.blogspot.ie/2013/03/the-brehon-law.html

Tierney J. (2009) Perspectives in Criminology Maidenhead: Open University Press.

Woods, Kieron (2011) The Irish Legal System [ONLINE] Last accessed 2 July 2012 http://irishbarrister.com/legalterms.html

Young, J. (1997), 'Left Realist Criminology: Radical in its Analysis, Realist in its Policy' in M. Maguire, R. Morgan & R. Reiner (eds), The Oxford Handbook of Criminology, Oxford: Oxford University Press

About the Author:

Teresa obtained her BA (Hons)LLB in 2005 she worked in legal investigations such as Miscarriage of Justice on behalf of clients who were either incarcerated or being charged with crimes they claimed they did not commit. She obtained a Masters in Criminology and Criminal Psychology in 2013 and has attended many seminars on criminal behaviour as well as numerous TV appearances.

An Irish writer of children's fiction and adults plain English legal and forensic psychology academic books. Teresa has been a private investigator, writer, photographer and lecturer, she backpacked around Europe with her daughter, sails a lovely boat called Baby Girl and survived a scuba diving accident.

A Law lecturer and Forensic Psychologist by profession Teresa moonlights as a Private "I" and Author, Teresa is as comfortable writing about magic, dragons and sorcerers as forensic psychology, criminology or the legal system. Teresa in a previous life was a photojournalist, having written for many local and national papers and magazines including the Mullingar Advertiser, Irish News Review, crime.ie and Emerald Road Racing.

Teresa is a registered member of the Teaching Council of Ireland. She has over 7 years' experience in teaching law and recognised the need for a beginners guide to law as she witnessed how the terminology and principles were hard work for some new students.

Teresa loves to read and has favourites in the classics such as Ulysses by James Joyce, Oliver Twist and David Copperfield by Charles Dickens, Roddy Doyle is a long term favourite of Teresa's. If you want to connect to Teresa you can go to http://www.facebook.com/cypathia; twitter @cypathia, or if you would like to know when Teresa's next book will come out, please visit her website at http://www.teresaclyne.com, where you can sign up to receive an email when she has her next release.

CPSIA information can be obtained
at www.ICGtesting.com
Printed in the USA
LVOW03s2241080616
491768LV00007B/272/P

9 781530 488148